Tell Me About God, Grandpa

God Bless You!

Smccoy

SHIRLEY MCCOY

ACKNOWLEDGEMENTS

With heartfelt thanks I praise God for His sovereign care in bringing into my life so many people who have encouraged me through their lives and actions, some unknowingly and others overtly. Even before thoughts of a book were in my mind, He was preparing the way. My special thanks to the following friends, and so many others who remain unnamed.

My affectionate thanks for my late husband, Bob. He became the prototype for Grandpa in *Tell Me about God, Grandpa*. His sunny disposition, sense of humor, and contagious laugh, along with his love of God and the Bible and his desire to teach people about both, were every bit as spontaneous and tangible as Grandpa's. And our dear friend, Judy Douglas, the most natural encourager I've ever known, has helped my life become more like the Grandma I'm still trying to become.

In 1983 I worked as secretary to the Missionary Board of the Brethren Church, whose seminary Bob was attending. One day, having read an article I had written for and about Brethren missionaries, someone named John Maust wrote me a short note asking if I had ever thought about writing. When I learned he was the Assistant Editor of *Christianity Today*, I felt so honored that I kept that note for years. Today, John is President of Media Associates International and travels internationally, encouraging and enabling Christian authors and publishers to "multiply themselves" by equipping others. His God-given gifts benefit many beyond myself in sharing our faith in, and love for, our wonderful Lord.

In 2010, Rev. Sam Bartlett, pastor of First Baptist Church, Galax, Virginia, introduced *Tell Me About God, Grandpa* to Vie Herlocker, editor of Sonfire Media. She phoned me and spent an hour talking with me, encouraging me to complete the work on it.

Several months later, after my move to Ocala, Florida, Amanda Williams, a member of Ocala First Baptist Church, who had written two Christian romance novellas, read part of the manuscript and gave me tips on publishing it, but I was not yet ready. Della Brock and Lois Lin, members of the same church, read the full manuscript and made every effort to find a publisher for the book, to no avail. But their cheering me on was a real blessing.

The 2013 Florida Christian Writers Conference and Word Weavers, International revived my desire to convey the book's thoughts to children. At the conference, I met one of the teachers, Cheri Cowell, who "just happened" to contact me when I was ready to step out in faith to publish this book.

Finally, exactly when needed, God providentially brought me together with Kay Forton, whose creative sketches add so much to the storyline. Just as amazingly, the Lord introduced me to Kim Shepson, who has spent hours diplomatically correcting my many errors with her proofreading abilities and patience. They and many others have helped me "birth" this book. I pray it will be a blessing to you. And may God be glorified

CONTENTS

	Acknowledgments	iii
Chapter 1	Fishing for Supper	7
Chapter 2	God Made Everything	11
Chapter 3	Simple Pleasures	15
Chapter 4	Teamwork	19
Chapter 5	A Friendship Walk	25
Chapter 6	A Sneaky Snake	31
Chapter 7	Picking Strawberries	35
Chapter 8	Homemade Ice Cream	39
Chapter 9	Friendship with God	43
Chapter 10	More Old-Fashioned Fun	47
Chapter 11	Potluck	51
Chapter 12	Smile, Jesus Loves You	53
Chapter 13	What Would Jesus Do?	59
Chapter 14	Sharing and Dreaming	61
	Addendum	65
	About the Author	73

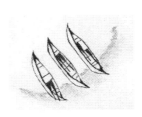

CHAPTER 1

FISHING FOR SUPPER

"I got one! I got one!" Joshua shouted with delight as he felt his fishing pole jerk and saw it bend toward the water.

Joshua's grandfather grabbed the fishing net and held it under Josh's line as he lifted the wiggling fish from its cold, wet home. "Looks like we can have some nice fresh fish for supper tonight," Grandpa said. "Shall we ask Grandma to fix it or shall I make a campfire and we can cook it out of doors?"

"O-o-o-h, let's cook outside! Then we can make s'mores for dessert. Oh, boy, I can hardly wait!"

Joshua and his grandfather picked up their fishing poles and bait and began the short walk to Grandma and Grandpa's place. Josh whistled a happy tune as they walked the block from the small lake to the camper home where Grandpa and Grandma spent their summers. Getting to spend his first week ever here without his mom and dad sure made him feel special.

As soon as they got to the camper, Joshua showed his catch to Grandma, and then Grandpa cleaned it and began making the campfire. It seemed like no time at all until Grandpa called, "Dinner's ready!" and Grandma had Joshua help her carry baked potatoes and corn-on-the-cob and a salad to the picnic table.

After they were all seated Grandpa and Grandma bowed their heads and Grandpa said a prayer to thank God for providing a great meal for them. How wonderful everything tasted! All of them agreed that no fish ever tasted as good as freshly caught fish cooked over a campfire. When Joshua got to make his own s'more with no help at all for the first time, he decided that being almost eight years old really made him feel like he was growing up.

Joshua helped his Grandma and Grandpa carry the dirty dishes into the camper. As Grandma washed and Joshua dried the dishes, Grandpa made sure the fire was completely out and then set up stakes so they could play a game of horseshoes. Josh loved playing this game. Even though he knew he couldn't pitch a horseshoe as far as Grandpa could, last year he had been able to throw almost as far as Grandma. He was eager to see if maybe, just maybe, he could beat her at least once this year. If he was really lucky he might even come close to tying with Grandpa.

"Do you think our yard's big enough to play horseshoes?" he asked his grandparents.

"Oh, I'm sure it is," said his grandmother. "Maybe that would be a good gift to ask for on your next birthday."

"That's just what I was thinking. I think all the guys that live near me would like pitchin' horseshoes. It'd be more fun than TV or computer games 'cause we'd be outside and get to use our muscles."

Grandpa and Grandma both laughed., "Would you believe we didn't even have TVs or computers when we were your age?" said Grandma.

"While you're here this week maybe you'd like to do some of the things with us that we used to do to have fun when we were kids. How does that sound?" Grandpa asked.

"Cool," Joshua said. "That sounds real cool. Sort of. I can't imagine what you could do that was fun before computers or televisions were made. Sounds to me like we might get bored quick."

"Well, we'll try not to let that happen," Grandpa chuckled.

After a few games of horseshoes Grandma suggested they all sit and watch the sun as it was setting for the night. How beautiful the sky looked with all the different shades of gold and red stretching as far right and left as they could see, and glowing softly as the sun disappeared below the horizon.

As it got darker and darker they noticed first one star and then another begin to sparkle above them. How black the night sky looked at first. But as they watched, more and more stars lit up the night sky. Joshua could hardly believe how many stars there were overhead! Grandma pointed out to him the stars that formed the Big Dipper.

"It's like a follow-the-dots picture in the sky!" Joshua exclaimed excitedly.

"Do you see the stars over there to the north that look like a large, spread-out 'W'?" Grandpa asked as he sketched the starry outline above them with his forefinger. That's a constellation known as Cassiopeia, or The Queen. There's a story in mythology that says she was such a beautiful goddess she got thrown into the sky, but because she became so proud, she was turned upside down part of the year to help rid her of her pride."

"What did you call that?"

"I'm not sure which thing you're asking about, but a group of stars that forms a picture is called a constellation. That constellation, known as The Queen, has the name Cassiopeia. And mythology is a collection of myths or make-believe stories from long, long ago. Any more questions?"

"Uh-huh. I can tell you were a teacher, Grandpa. That reminded me of something Mrs. Underwood would have said in science class. But I do have a question: Why don't I see these at home? We go out in our backyard for cookouts, too, but I've never noticed so many stars at one time before."

"You live in a city, and the lights of all the big buildings and signs and houses, and cars and trucks and buses, make so much light that the light from the stars can't be seen. Out here there isn't much in the way of light, so the stars can be seen in all their glory."

"Wow! Neat!" Rubbing his neck as he adjusted his gaze from the spectacular stars to their little campsite, Joshua saw the off-and-on blinking of fireflies. "It's almost like they're trying to light up the yard the way the stars light up the sky," he said, smiling at the thought.

"If you'd like, the night before you leave for home you can catch some of those lightning bugs to take with you," Grandma said. "How does that sound?"

Trying to stifle a yawn, Joshua nodded his head. "Sounds great," he said and smiled sleepily.

Noticing his drowsiness, Grandpa stood up. "Time for a bath and bedtime before your Grandma and I fall asleep out here and you have to carry us both to bed." He laughed a hearty laugh and Joshua giggled as he pictured that happening. Then Grandpa took Joshua's hand in his, put his other arm around Grandma, and together they walked toward the camper.

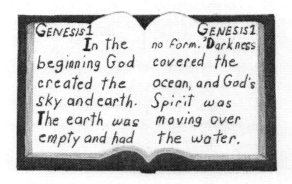

CHAPTER 2

GOD MADE EVERYTHING

The next morning Joshua laid in bed trying to decide if Grandma and Grandpa were awake yet. Hearing no sounds coming from the kitchen, he tiptoed in that direction.

As he looked into the front room he saw Grandpa sitting in his favorite chair with a book open in his lap. "Whatcha readin', Grandpa?" he asked.

"My favorite book, the Bible," Grandpa answered with a smile on his face that told Joshua his grandpa was really enjoying it.

"What's it about?" Joshua questioned.

"It's about God. And every time I read it I learn more about him. It's full of stories, but they aren't make-believe stories like lots of books have. They're stories about things that really happened. Like how the earth was made. Or about real people--like Noah, who built a huge boat to keep animals safe in during a flood. Or Daniel, who was thrown into a large hole in the ground that had lions in it, but God kept them from hurting him. And Jesus, God's Son, who came to teach people about God and show us how much He loves us."

"That sounds awesome, Grandpa. Will you read me some of those stories? And can you tell me about God, Grandpa?"

"Josh, there's nothing I'd enjoy more than telling you about God. I have an idea! Remember last night how Grandma and I said we'd do something different every day while you're here that she and I used to do for fun with our friends when we were young?"

"Yeah, but how does that tell me about God?"

"It doesn't. I thought that maybe, just like when we decided to do that, you might like to hear about God a little each day, too.

"Sounds good to me. But could I have some cereal, please?" Joshua asked.

"Of course! Think I'll have some with you." Grandpa said as he got a couple of boxes of cereal for Joshua to choose from. "And how about some orange juice?"

"Okay!" Joshua said as he dropped into a table-side chair. "I know you're not looking at your Bible, but could you tell me one of those Bible stories while we're eating breakfast?"

"Absolutely!" Grandpa responded enthusiastically. "In fact, while I was going to sleep last night I was thinking about how much the three of us enjoyed looking at the stars. Well, God made those stars."

"No kidding!" Joshua exclaimed, stopping his spoon halfway to his mouth. "How did He do that?"

"He only needed to speak and they were created. He also made the earth we live on and everything on it. In fact, there's nothing that exists, nothing you can see or hear, that wasn't made by Him. And that's why we call Him our Creator."

"He even made fireflies?"

"Yep!"

"And cats and dogs?"

"Yes, cats and dogs, too."

"And bugs and bears and butterflies, and . . . "

"Absolutely! Anything you can think of was made by God. He even made the food we eat and the air we breathe."

"Awesome!" Joshua had resumed eating, though he obviously was impressed. "Did He make this cereal we're eating?"

"Well, not exactly. But God made the grain, and the sugar beets, or sugar cane, and other ingredients that people used to make it. And if He hadn't done that we couldn't be eating it."

"Did He make you and Grandma and me and all the other people, too?"

"That's sort of like what I told you about the cereal. Although it takes a man and a woman to make a baby, God is the one who made the first man and woman so they could have children. And from those first two people, Adam and Eve, all of us have eventually been born."

"Sounds like I'm missing out on quite a discussion," Grandma said as she walked into the kitchen and began to make coffee.

"Grandpa was just telling me about things God created," Joshua spoke up excitedly. "Did you know that He made EVERYTHING?"

"I sure did!" Grandma replied. "Isn't our Heavenly Father wonderful?"

"Our Heavenly Father? Who is that?" Joshua asked. "I thought Grandpa was telling me about God."

Grandma leaned over and kissed Joshua on the top of his head. "Actually, 'Heavenly Father' is just one of the names people use when they talk about God. His Son, Jesus, called Him that and let us know we can, too, because God loves us, just like all good fathers love their children."

"Neat! So in a way I have two fathers!"

"Yes, the one you've always known, whom your mommy is married to, and also your Father in heaven, who is God. Do you remember the picture we have of you when you were real little, and you were standing in a pair of your daddy's shoes? You wanted so much to be like him," Grandma said, smiling as she pictured one of her favorite snapshots of Joshua. "Your dad was so proud when you tried to imitate him. And now you watch your dad and do a lot of things he does."

"You know, God would like His children to see what He's like, and then be like Him, too. It makes Him proud and happy if you imitate Him, just like it makes your dad feel when you try to do what he does."

Joshua squinted as he tried to figure it out. "But how can I be like God when I can't see Him?"

"Good question, Joshua! And the answer is that we can see what God is like by reading the Bible," Grandpa chimed in.

"Do they have pictures of Him in there?"

"They don't have pictures like you put in a frame, but they have what you could call 'word pictures.' They don't show us what He looks like, but they tell us what He's like. They tell us He's good, and wise, and patient, and fair, and forgiving. We learn that God never lies or breaks a promise. He also knows what's in our hearts," Grandma added. "But there's so much more that word pictures tell us about God that I think maybe we should wait until tomorrow for that. We want to get dressed and do one of those old-time things before it gets too hot."

"All right!" Joshua shouted as he jumped up from the table. "I'll be the first one ready to go!"

"Honey," Grandpa lowered his voice after Josh left the room, "maybe Joshua's parents won't be pleased when they learn that we've talked to him about Jesus."

"I've thought about that, and you may be right," she sighed. "But look how eager he is to learn about God and the Bible. We can pray his parents will be, too."

"Of course. I should have thought of that," Grandpa said as he reached for her hand and began to pray. "Father, we know you love Joshua even more than we do, and we're thankful that you also love his parents. We're so pleased you're giving us the joy of telling him about you. We ask you to work in his mom's and dad's hearts to join him in the desire to know more about you and your wonderful plan for their lives. Thank you for this day with Joshua and help us to recognize the opportunities you give us to share your love with him and others. In Jesus' name. Amen."

CHAPTER 3

SIMPLE PLEASURES

It was mid-morning when Grandpa, Grandma and Joshua arrived at the small building where canoes could be rented. "Just a two-hour rental, please," Grandpa told the young person in charge.

"Thank you, sir," she answered politely as she took his money and pointed the three of them to where several canoes lay waiting. Grandpa and Grandma looked at a few of the canoes and then chose a cheerful orange one. The young lady who had rented the canoe cautioned them, "Be sure to put on your life jackets before you leave."

"Should we go if it's dangerous?" Joshua asked.

"Good thinking," Grandma said, "but where we'll be going there's not much to worry about. We won't be hitting rough water or making our way around big tree roots or big rocks. We just thought you might like an idea of what it's like to do some canoeing. That's something we used to do a lot when we were teenagers."

"Very cool," Joshua said as they each put on a life jacket. Then he and Grandma got in the canoe before Grandpa shoved it away from the shore and jumped in.

Joshua sat up front, Grandma was on the middle seat, and Grandpa was doing all the paddling from the back of the canoe. After a few minutes Grandma turned around and said to Grandpa, "How about handing me one of those paddles?"

Grandpa leaned forward carefully and held out a paddle to Grandma. "Which side do you want to paddle on?" he asked.

"The left, if that's okay with you," she replied over her shoulder.

"Okay, let's show our grandson how to get a little more speed out of one of these," Grandpa said as Grandma began rowing in rhythm with him.

To Joshua's surprise the canoe really did pick up speed with two people paddling instead of one. "Can I try it? Can I?" he pleaded with them.

"Let us keep the rhythm going for a while so you can get the feel of what you need to do when you take my place," Grandma suggested.

After what seemed to Josh like forever, Grandpa asked, "Think you've got the picture?"

"I sure do! Just give me your paddle, Grandma!"

Joshua stood up, swung around quickly, and reached back for the paddle. He froze in mid-air when he felt the canoe tilt from side to side. "What did I do wrong?" he asked with alarm, afraid to move a muscle.

"It's okay, don't worry. It just shows you how little it takes to tip a canoe. But as long as you're careful and don't move too quickly we'll be fine," Grandpa assured him.

Joshua grasped the paddle Grandma held out to him, eased down onto his seat, and began his turn helping Grandpa paddle the canoe. At first his strokes seemed to just skim the top of the water. "It's not as easy as it looks," he said. "How do you do this?"

"Try to hold the paddle a little more up and down instead of so flat," called Grandpa. "I'll slow down a little and we'll see if that helps." And it did.

Joshua was delighted to feel himself actually paddling the canoe with his Grandpa. He felt so excited he would have liked to jump up and down. But he remembered how the canoe had tipped back and forth when all he had done was stand to reach back for the paddle. He decided he'd wait until he was on dry ground to do the jumping up and down.

How quiet things were as the canoe slipped almost silently through the water. Not many other people seemed to be taking advantage of the beautiful day to spend time on the lake. It was nice to have this part of it almost to themselves.

It wasn't long before Joshua found himself wearing out. "My arms are getting tired," he said with disappointment.

"You've been doing real well but I wondered how long you could keep it up. Would you like me to take over again for a while?" Grandma offered.

"Can I have a turn again before we have to take the canoe back?"

"Sure," Grandma said with a smile. "Just hand the paddle back to me and I'll take your place for a little bit."

This time the trade went more smoothly and she and Grandpa resumed their rhythmical paddling.

"Now that you're not busy paddling you can relax and look around," Grandpa suggested to Joshua. "Did you notice that it's cooler when we go under the shade of a tree? And did you see how many different creatures enjoy being along the edges of the lake?"

"Guess I wasn't paying attention to anything but trying to learn how to paddle," Joshua said as he bit into the apple he had brought along and began to look around. "Look at that bird with long legs, standing on only one foot over there. He looks so funny!" Joshua laughed out loud and was surprised to see the bird fly away at the sound of his laughter. "Oops, I didn't mean to scare him. Sorry, bird."

"That was a whooping crane," Grandpa informed him.

It wasn't long before Joshua noticed how it really did feel cooler as they passed into the shade of a huge tree that bordered the lake and then warmed up again as soon as its shadow no longer protected them. "Cool," he whispered, as though he thought speaking might shatter the pleasure of it all.

"Would you like to just float without rowing for a while, and enjoy the quiet for a bit?" Grandpa offered after they had made the turn.

"I'd love it," Grandma answered.

"So would I," chorused Joshua.

Grandpa and Grandma both drew their paddles into the canoe and it drifted to almost a standstill. Not even one other canoe was in sight now. Joshua closed his eyes and listened to the sounds around them. Somewhere off in the distance he heard the faint sound of a car horn. And a dog barking. Then he heard nothing but the rustle of a light breeze in the leaves of a tree on the shoreline. A nearby splash surprised him, but Grandpa said it probably was just the sound of a fish dropping back into the water after a big jump. Or it might have been a frog.

Joshua opened his eyes and looked around. First he saw another of those birds standing on one leg. What had Grandpa said they were? Oh, yeah, whooping cranes. Then he spotted three chipmunks that looked like they were playing tag. He would have laughed out loud at the chipmunks, but he remembered how his laugh had scared the whooping crane away earlier, so he put his hand over his mouth just in time. What else might he see?

He looked overhead and spied two smaller birds gliding on the wind's currents. As he lowered his gaze he noticed the lovely blue of some flowers that grew close to the ground, and a cluster of bulrushes hugging the bank of the lake. Two ducks were lazily floating in the shadow of the bulrushes. Then, looking even more closely, he noticed there were several baby ducklings almost hidden in the shadows right behind them, following their parents like mirror images. "How cool!" he thought.

"Are you okay, Josh?" Grandpa asked.

"Uh-huh. I was just trying to take a picture with my mind so I can remember this forever," Joshua said quietly. "I wish I could paint a picture that would look like this. I know you told me this morning that God created everything. He sure did a good job, didn't He?"

"Absolutely!" Grandma and Grandpa said at the same time.

Grandpa glanced at his watch. "Looks like we need to be turning around soon so we can get this canoe back before our two hours are over," he said as he picked up his paddle. "Let's make a turn to the left just after we pass that tree. Okay, Dear?

"Okay, Honey," Grandma answered as she rejoined him in their rhythmical rowing.

Suddenly it occurred to Joshua that they were actually returning the canoe and, if he didn't hurry, soon his opportunity to row any more would be gone. "Hey, can I have my second turn now?" he asked.

This time the transfer of the paddle between Grandma and Joshua went so smoothly you would have thought the three of them had canoed together for a long time. Joshua was surprised and pleased that he was able to help with the paddling all the way to where they needed to drop off the canoe. As Grandpa steered it into the bank of the lake, he asked Josh "Do you think you could hop out and pull the canoe a little farther forward onto the land while I push us a little ahead with my paddle?"

"Sure, Grandpa," Joshua said confidently as he gingerly made his way the few steps to the front of the canoe, eased himself onto the wet, muddy ground, and then picked up the rope and tugged as hard as he could while Grandpa used the paddle to push. Joshua tied the best knot he knew how around the pole just ahead of them.

"Great job, my boy," Grandpa said proudly as he got out of the canoe and turned to help Grandma climb out, too. "Just let me tie that knot a little more securely and we'll be ready to go. Did you enjoy yourself?"

"Did I ever! It was so cool that if we didn't even do any more old-fashioned things it would be okay. But I hope we will, because I can hardly wait to see what other neat stuff you and Grandma did in the good old days."

"Three more days to do at least three more old-fashioned things," Grandpa said. "Think we can come up with that many old-timey ideas, Grandma?"

Grandma looked at Grandpa and then at Joshua, and with a twinkle in her eyes, but without saying a word, she smiled a great big smile at both of them.

"Now I can hardly wait for tomorrow!" Joshua said excitedly as he ran toward the car.

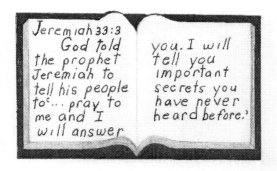

Jeremiah 33:3
God told the prophet Jeremiah to tell his people to^c... pray to me and I will answer you. I will tell you important secrets you have never heard before.'

CHAPTER 4

TEAMWORK

Joshua woke the next morning to the soft pitter-patter of rain. "Oh, no," he thought, "there's no way we can have fun today with it raining." He threw back his covers, slid out of bed, and hurried toward where he knew he would find Grandpa reading his Bible. Grandma was also there with a Bible in her lap, much to his surprise. "I didn't know you both liked to read the Bible," he said.

"It's my favorite book, too," Grandma replied.

"She probably could tell you as much about God as I can," Grandpa added. "It looks like we'll be staying inside for a while this morning. Maybe after we have breakfast we could both help you learn more about God."

"Speaking of breakfast, how would a vegetable omelet, and some toast, and tomato juice sound to you this morning?" Grandma asked.

Grandpa and Joshua agreed with that menu before she could offer an alternative. As Grandma began to break eggs into a dish, Grandpa began dicing red and green peppers, mushrooms, and onions. Joshua filled three glasses with tomato juice. "Can I make the toast, too?" he asked.

"Sure!" Grandma answered as she whipped a little water into the eggs to help make the omelet light and fluffy. "Are the veggies ready?" she asked Grandpa.

"All ready. Shall I cook this morning and you do dishes, or do you want to cook and I'll do dishes?"

"Why don't we let you cook, and then you and Joshua can set up a board game while I do dishes."

"Okay," Grandpa agreed as he grabbed a big skillet, sprayed it with cooking oil, set it on the largest burner, and then poured the egg mixture in after the skillet was warm enough. After the eggs had cooked a bit, Grandpa poured the vegetables onto one half of them, slid a broad spatula underneath the other half and folded those eggs over on top of the vegetables.

Joshua's eyes lit up with anticipation. "Wow!" he exclaimed.

A couple minutes later, Grandpa made a quick move forward with the skillet, then up and back, and the omelet flipped over in the air all by itself. As it was falling, Grandpa reached under the omelet with the skillet just in time to catch it and return it to the burner. "That was awesome, Grandpa!" Josh said as Grandpa smiled with obvious delight at his admirer.

"Showoff!" Grandma teased. "He knows I can't do that, and it's another reason I had him cook this morning. I thought you'd enjoy that, Joshua."

"It was awesome! Oh, should I put the bread in the toaster now?"

"Great idea! And while Grandpa cuts the omelet into three pieces I'll get some shredded cheese to sprinkle on it, and then breakfast will be ready."

"Looks like we make a pretty good team in the kitchen, just like we did in the canoe," Grandpa commented as they all sat down to eat. "Now let's thank the Lord for this great-looking food."

The three of them closed their eyes and bowed their heads as Grandpa prayed. "We give you thanks, Father, for blessing us with food that helps us to be healthy and happy, and tastes delicious, and for the joy we had working together to prepare it. You are so kind and good, and we love you for blessing us so much. Amen."

"Grandpa, why do we pray before we eat?" Joshua questioned as he buttered his toast.

Let me answer your question by asking you a question," Grandpa replied. "If I did nice things for you, would you thank me?"

"Sure!"

"Remember that yesterday we talked about God making everything?"

"Uh-huh."

"Well, that includes the things that go into all that we eat-- just like we talked about when you were eating your cereal yesterday, remember?"

"Uh-huh."

"So why not thank our Father in heaven for being nice to us by giving us such delicious things to eat?"

"Oh, I see. But does He really listen to us when we do that?"

"He certainly does. He listens whenever we talk to Him. Your Grandma and I talk to Him every day. Some days we even talk to Him lots of different times."

"But what is there to talk about?" Joshua inquired as he pierced a big bite of omelet with his fork.

"Just about anything you can think of. After we read our Bibles, we might spend half an hour talking to God. We might thank Him for something we especially appreciated reading. We could thank Him for the beautiful day and good health. Then we might pray for people we know who are sick; and for missionaries. They're people who often go to other countries to tell people about God and Jesus. Of course we always pray for our kids and grandkids."

"That's nice," Joshua interjected with a smile.

Grandpa smiled back at him, took a swallow of his juice, and continued. "Sometimes we ask God to forgive our country for some things it has done that weren't things that would please Him. Or we might thank Him for our freedom, and ask Him to bless our men and women in the military, and our President and other people who govern our country. Oh, my, I could tell you even more that we pray about, but I think you get the idea."

"Yeah, I think so. But how do you know He even listens to what you and Grandma say?"

"Grandma, we don't mean to be leaving you out of this. Why don't you answer that question for Joshua?" Grandpa replied as he began eating again.

"Joshua, two things prove to us God listens. One is that the Bible tells us He does. A lot of verses tell us that, but probably my favorite is Jeremiah 33:3. God told the prophet Jeremiah to tell His people to '. . . pray to Me, and I will answer you. I will tell you important secrets you have never heard before.' The other way that we know is that we have seen God answer prayers many times."

"That's awesome," Joshua said. "But I have a friend, Gabe--he's my best friend. mother got cancer last year and he prayed for her but she died. And I don't get it. If God answers your prayers why didn't He answer Gabe's? He had a neat mom. I'd be mad, too, if what happened to his mom happened to mine. I'm not sure I'd even want to talk to God. Why did God let her die?

"That's a real good question, Joshua. Even a lot of grown-ups wonder about things like that. Some of them have gotten angry with God, too, and given up learning about Him because they couldn't figure it out," Grandma said. "If people have never really understood what an awesome God He is in so many ways, it's no wonder they've given up."

"What we believe is that most people have never learned about what great character God has," Grandpa chimed in.

"Huh? What does that mean?" asked Joshua, who had barely noticed that he and his grandparents had all finished eating.

21

Grandma nodded to Grandpa that she would be glad to let him talk as she removed the dishes that now sat empty in front of them. "Your character is who you are," he explained. "It has a lot to do with your mind, your feelings, and your actions. If you were to describe someone you know, without talking about their looks, you would be telling us about their character. Are they angry a lot, or are they patient? Do they think about others first, or are they selfish? If they are strong, do they use their strength to help others or to hurt them? Do their actions show them to be smart or not?"

"How did you learn all those kinds of things about God?" Joshua asked as he gazed out the sliding glass door at the rain pelting the neighbor's colorful variety of flowers.

"That's one reason we enjoy reading the Bible so much," Grandma replied as she washed the dishes. "God wants us to know Him, so He had many different people write many different things to help us learn about Him."

"I still don't understand how knowing that helps," Joshua confessed.

"Do you think you know me pretty well?" asked Grandpa.

"Sure. That's a silly question."

"If someone told you that I had stolen their lawn mower would you believe them?"

"Of course not!"

"If someone said I had told them a lie, what would you think?"

"They made a mistake, 'cause you don't tell lies."

"What if they said they saw me hit Grandma, what about that?"

"You would never hit Grandma! You love her too much!" Joshua replied defensively.

"That's exactly right," Grandpa said with a broad smile. "But how can you be so sure about those things?"

"Because I know you!" Joshua said emphatically.

"That's exactly what we're saying. You know my character. And from reading the Bible and talking with God in prayer and watching Him answer prayer, we know His character. Because of that we've learned we can trust Him. If we don't get the answer we hoped and prayed for it's because He has something better in mind."

"But I think if I tried to tell Gabe that, he'd probably be mad at me and never want me to talk to him again," Josh responded. He scanned the skies quickly, looking hopefully for a glimpse of sunshine around the edge of one of the dark clouds.

"It's possible that Gabe would be angry," Grandpa continued, "but if you feel strongly that Gabe needs your help and God's help, then you can begin asking God to give you the right time and the right way to talk to him. And as you keep showing Gabe that you care about him, God will give you an opportunity."

"Well, guys, I'm through doing dishes," Grandma said. "If you're ready to move on to other things, I'll get out some old games, since it's still raining. Hopefully it will stop raining so we won't have to forget about the walk we want to take around the campground tonight."

"Only one more thing first, Honey," Grandpa said. "Let's pray for Joshua's friend before we start playing games, okay?"

"Of course. I'm glad you thought of that," she answered, and bowed her head.

"Father God," Grandpa prayed, "we are so glad you've given Joshua a caring heart for his friend Gabe's problem. We know You want Gabe to come to know You and experience the help he needs to get over the pain of his mother's death. Please help him see that Joshua cares about his hurting. And give Joshua the opportunity to talk to him about you and your love for him and for his mother. In Jesus' Name. Amen."

"Thank you, Grandpa. I'm so glad to be here. I'm having such a good time. And I'm glad you can tell me things about God."

"And now to the games," Grandma said as she entered the kitchen and placed a stack of boxes on the table.

B	I	N	G	O
4	22	38	49	74
13	20	42	60	69
6	18	FRee space	50	73
1	30	45	54	61
15	27	40	52	70

TELL ME ABOUT GOD, GRANDPA

CHAPTER 5

A FRIENDSHIP WALK

"Checkers. Dominoes. Bingo. Old Maid." Joshua counted on his fingers as he named the games they had played. "Oh, and Chinese Checkers, too. That makes at least five games. Did I miss any?"

"Well, I don't remember for sure," said Grandpa, "but I enjoyed the teasing and the laughing even more than the games. I see it's stopped raining. I'd love to go out and stretch my legs. Anyone want to go with me?"

"I do!" Joshua exclaimed and headed for the door.

The rest of the day passed as quickly as the morning had. "This has been another great day," Josh observed after they finished their evening meal. "Didn't you say something about taking a walk tonight? Why is that old-fashioned? My mom and dad take lots of power walks."

"Aha! That's it." Grandpa told him. "There are power walks and there are friendship walks. You know what a power walk is about: it's to help you stay or get healthy. But a friendship walk--well, let's just take ours and you can see for yourself. They're both good for you, but boy are they different! Let me grab our flashlight before we go because it might be dark by the time we head back home."

When they left home, Grandpa and Grandma walked right down the middle of their street. "Don't do that. You're going to get run over!" Joshua begged as he kept to the grassy areas. Much to his surprise they both laughed at him.

"Take a look around," Grandpa told him. "How many cars do you see moving here in the campground?"

Joshua took a quick glance around them and realized he only saw one car being driven, and that was a couple of streets away.

Grandma pointed to a sign they were passing with "20 mph" written on it in large numbers.

"Oh," Joshua observed. "Not many people driving and you can't drive more than twenty miles an hour. No wonder you weren't worried. And no wonder there aren't sidewalks here, either. People can walk in the streets safely."

"We do keep our ears open, because once in a while there will be someone who isn't used to that speed limit and doesn't notice they're going too fast. But everyone walks leisurely on the road. And notice what else they do," Grandma said as she waved to a lady sitting on her front porch and called out to her, "How did that pie recipe work for you, Edith?"

"Best chocolate pie I ever made," Edith replied. "Thanks so much! The ladies I play bridge with loved it."

A little farther down the road Grandpa began a conversation with a man mowing his lawn. The man had stopped his mower when he saw them approaching, and Grandpa walked a little faster, moving ahead to shake hands with him. Grandpa greeted him with a question, "Hey, Herb, I see you got your mower fixed. What did you find was wrong with it?"

"Oh, the spark plug and the air filter needed cleaned; that was all. It's running fine now."

"Glad to hear it. I'd like you to meet our grandson, Joshua. He's spending the week with us, and we're enjoying every minute of it."

"Joshua, this is Mister McCoy. The McCoys are from Ohio."

"I'm glad to meet you, young man," Mr. McCoy said as he extended his large hand to give Joshua's firm handshake.

"Thank you, sir. I'm glad to meet you, too. I don't know just where Ohio is, but I've heard of the Ohio State Buckeyes. Did you ever see them play?"

"Yep, a couple times. Not a bad team. My wife likes to go to their games because she thinks they've got a great band."

"So do I," Grandma offered. "And where is Jane this evening?"

"Oh, she's out walking, too. She grabbed her harmonica and said something about heading for the Johnsons' place. I'll probably go over there when I finish working on our yard," Mr. McCoy said.

"That's good to hear! We'll walk over that way now. Hope to see you later."

When they got to the next corner they turned left and soon crossed paths with two ladies walking the opposite direction, each with a dog on a leash. They stopped to pet the dogs and chat with the ladies for a few minutes, and an older couple riding a bicycle built for two rode by and said "hi" to them.

At the following corner Grandma and Grandpa stopped to talk with a little old lady trimming her plants as her husband sat in a wheelchair watching. "Your roses are looking so lovely, Frances," Grandma encouraged her as they passed.

"Thank you so much, dear. It's a lovely evening to be outside working."

"And walking," Grandma added with a warm smile. "Hi, Frank! It's nice to see you're able to be outside tonight, too," she added, with a wave to Frances's husband as they walked on by.

"Do you guys know everyone?" Joshua asked, emphasizing the last word of his question.

"No, not all the folks, but quite a few of them. That's why we call our walks friendship walks," Grandpa explained. "But you could call them old-fashioned walks, because as we were growing up families often took walks in the evening. There wasn't air conditioning then, and getting outside was a good way to enjoy the slowly cooling outdoor air and visit with your neighbors at the same time."

By this time they arrived at the last camper on the street, where several people were sitting out front. Two guys were tuning their guitars while a lady was tuning her fiddle to them. Joshua figured the lady with the harmonica in her hand must be Mr. McCoy's wife. He guessed there must be a dozen or more other people there, all talking comfortably with one another. He liked just listening to the sound of their happy chatter. Some of the people sat on lawn chairs scattered here and there, others sat on blankets they had brought, while still others stood around. Grandma, Grandpa, and Josh eased themselves into three empty chairs that were front and center in the small group.

Soon one of the guitarists said, "One, two, three," and without any music to read, the four of them played a peppy old tune. One person began clapping in time with the music and soon everyone was clapping their hands or tapping their toes as the song drew them together with its enthusiastic beat.

As soon as the music was over, one of the men who was listening called out, "How about playing, 'When the Saints Come Marching In?'" Joshua saw the musicians look at each other, nod, and begin the lively tune.

"I wonder if they know 'Yankee Doodle,'" Joshua said to his grandparents, hoping their answer would be "yes."

"I'm sure they'll be glad to play it if they know it. Go ahead and ask when they finish this song," Grandma suggested.

But when that song ended, a lady called out the name of another old song. Then another person wanted a country music song; and a person he didn't see requested an old hymn. Joshua wondered if he would ever get to ask about "Yankee Doodle." Then he had an idea. As soon as the group finished playing he jumped to his feet and shouted, "Do you know 'Yankee Doodle?'"

The little group of musicians looked at one another and nodded. But before the lead guitarist began to play, he surprised Joshua by saying, "If you can sing it, we can play it."

Josh looked wide-eyed at his grandparents. He never thought that he might have to sing in front of these strangers. Then he saw his grandparents nodding and smiling at him and looked around at the other people and saw them nodding and smiling, too. "Okay," he said, "I'll try, but I'm not sure I know all the words."

"If you have a problem, we'll help you along," the lead guitarist assured him. "We're not auditioning for *American Idol* here, we're just enjoying ourselves." With that he began playing "Yankee Doodle," and sang softly to help Joshua get started. Before the first verse was over, Joshua was pleased to find himself singing as though he were alone in his own room. "This isn't as bad as I thought it would be," he told himself as he kept singing.

As he sang the last note, everyone clapped their hands with delight. Joshua felt his face getting warm and knew he must be blushing, but he could see how proud his grandparents looked when he returned to his seat. "Wow! Something else to tell my parents and friends when I get home," he thought.

For probably another half hour the band played one old song after another. It was amazing how much music those people knew. But soon, just as people had arrived one- by-one or two-by-two, they began to drift away. Grandpa and Grandma looked at each other and agreed it was time for them to be heading home, too.

On the way back to the camper, Joshua could see why Grandpa had stopped to grab his flashlight before they left--the campground didn't have streetlights. He hadn't noticed that before. There were a few lights here and there from outside lights on people's motor homes or campers, but sometimes the street was unlit for several homes in a row. It would have been easy to trip over something you didn't see in the road. Grandpa had Grandma take hold of his arm and Joshua held her other hand as they all walked with the flashlight illuminating the road a little bit ahead of them.

"This makes me think of a Bible verse. Can you guess which one?" Grandpa asked Grandma.

"I was just thinking of that," Grandma answered. "Psalm 119:105, 'Your word is like a lamp for my feet and a light for my path.'"

"I don't get it," Joshua said. "How can the Bible be a lamp or a light?"

"You see how this flashlight is showing us things that could cause us to fall if we didn't see them?" Grandpa asked.

"Uh-huh."

"We can also shine it ahead of us and see where the next corner is so we know where to make a turn, can't we?"

"Uh-huh."

"The Bible tells us how to live the way God wants us to so we can recognize things that might cause us to stumble in life and get hurt. It also can teach us how to look ahead and change the path we're taking if a different way to go would be better for us."

"Oh, I see. Sort of like a GPS, isn't it?"

"You've got the idea, all right," Grandpa said. "Very good."

"I see we're almost home," Grandma noticed. "The trip goes a lot faster when we don't stop to talk to people along the way, doesn't it?"

"Yeah, but it was nice to see your neighbors on the way there. Now when I'm at home and think of you, I can picture some of your friends, too," Joshua told them. "Before we go in, can we take time to see if I can find those stars that make up that picture in the sky? What did you call it?"

"A constellation," Grandpa replied. "Do you remember the two we looked at the other night?" he asked as he turned off the flashlight.

"Right up there is the spread-out 'W' that I remember you called The Queen, but I don't remember what her name was. And over there is the Big Dipper." Joshua proudly pointed to both of the constellations he had learned about earlier.

Grandma informed him that The Queen's name was Cassiopeia. With a quick hug she mentioned that if they wanted to have the old-time adventure of berry picking tomorrow, they better head for showers and bed so they could be rested for their fun time in the morning. "If you've never been berry picking before, I think you're in for a treat," she promised.

"Oh, boy!" Joshua exclaimed. "Another old-time adventure. I'm glad you had so many different things to do when you were growing up. No wonder you didn't have computers or TVs. You had too many fun things to keep you busy to even need them."

"Well, I've never thought of it that way before," Grandpa chuckled. "But it's an interesting way to end the day."

And turning the flashlight on again so they could see their way into the camper, he breathed a small prayer. "Thank You, Lord, for another day in your beautiful world, and for the blessing of another day with our grandson. May He continue to seek you with all his heart forever."

Tree of the Knowledge of Good and Evil

CHAPTER 6

A SNEAKY SNAKE

Even with the blinds closed, the sun filtering into the room woke Joshua. He could smell coffee, so he knew he wasn't the first one awake today. After stretching and yawning he sprang from bed and made tracks for the front room.

This time it was Grandma who was sitting in her chair alone with her Bible in front of her. She was underlining something on the page she held open.

"What do you do that for?" Josh asked.

"When I really like something I read, I like to be able to find it more quickly. Underlining helps me do that."

"You and Grandpa really like God and the Bible, don't you?"

"You bet! Would you like me to tell you a couple of things about God while your grandfather is getting dressed?

"I remember He's our Creator, and heavenly Father, and that He listens to us. And if He doesn't answer a prayer, it's because He has something better for us. Is there more to learn than that?"

"If I were your teacher I'd give you an 'A' for that answer. There is more to learn, though. Your grandpa and I are still enjoying learning. Maybe knowing that God is wise would be another thing you'd like to know."

"You mean He's smart?"

"Oh, He's that all right, but it's more than that. Let's pretend you did something wrong while you're here and Grandpa and I found out about it. After we talked to you about it, we might discipline you because of what you did. As much as we would want to discipline you correctly, we might somehow just not make the right decision. But when God disciplines a person He knows exactly the right way to correct them. He doesn't make mistakes like people do.

"First, He forgives that person if they ask Him to. Always there is His forgiveness, but sometimes He knows it is also good for that person to receive discipline. The Bible tells us He disciplines those He loves."

"Why does He do that?"

"When God disciplines a person it's to give them an opportunity to learn. God is trying to help them change the way they are doing something so they can become better--more like His Son, Jesus."

"Oh. I see why you and Grandpa like to read about God so much," Joshua said, "but why don't other people? Mom and Dad don't read the Bible and they don't pray. And neither does anyone else I know. But after you've told me about Him this week, I'd think everyone would want to be a friend of God and have Him be their friend."

Grandpa had walked into the room as Joshua was expressing himself. "We can tell you a little about why your mom is that way, since we're her parents," he explained. "She didn't grow up hearing about God because she was an adult before anyone told Grandma and me about becoming Christians and learning about God. So we didn't know how important it was while she was growing up. Now she's married and has you and your dad and a job and just seems too busy to make the time to go to church or to read the Bible."

"But I think she'd like to know the things you've been telling me."

"You know, Josh, we'd love to tell her, and at times we've tried, but she seems to think we're treating her like she's a kid. We don't want to hurt her feelings, so we just keep praying for God to reach her, and your dad, in some other way."

"I wish I knew how to tell them, but I don't know the things about God and the Bible like you do," Joshua said.

"You two just gave me an idea," Grandma interrupted excitedly. "When we take you home on Saturday we could tell your parents that you've asked us about God. And we could let them know that we've given you some Bible verses that tell about what we've talked about, so if they were interested they could read them, too."

"Oh, could you? Would you?" Joshua asked, obviously very pleased with the idea.

"While you and Grandpa find something to do this afternoon, I'll be glad to look up some verses and get them ready for you. Right now, if you two will excuse me, I thought I'd make some waffles for breakfast."

So while Grandma busied herself in the kitchen, Grandpa explained to Joshua a little bit about how the Bible is divided into two parts. "The first section is called the Old Testament," he began. "Everything in it happened before Jesus was born. And in the very first Old Testament book, Genesis, it tells about God creating the heavens and the earth. It also tells about God creating plants and trees; the sun, moon and stars; fish and birds and animals; and finally creating Adam and then Eve.

"Adam and Eve were the first of all the men and women who have ever been on earth," Grandpa continued. "And God placed them in a beautiful garden known as the Garden of Eden. He told them they could eat from any tree or plant in Eden, except from the Tree of the Knowledge of Good and Evil. But there was a snake in that garden and--wait a minute! Let me interrupt myself to ask you if you've ever heard of Satan."

"Isn't he someone who's wicked or mean or bad? I think he's in some stories, but I'm not sure if he's real, though."

"Oh, he's real all right. In fact, at one time he was an angel and lived in heaven. But he got very proud and wanted to be like God, so God threw him out of heaven and he ended up on earth."

"No kidding?"

"No kidding. Anyway, now that you know he's real, let me continue with the story about Adam and Eve. One day Satan disguised himself as a snake and he slithered over to Eve and had a conversation with her."

"Really? The snake could talk?"

"Yes, somehow Satan made a tempting voice come from that snake and it said to Eve, 'Has God said you shouldn't eat from every tree of the garden?'"

Joshua almost laughed because Grandpa sounded so funny trying to sound like he thought a snake would sound if it could talk, but Josh didn't want to interrupt the story.

Then Grandpa tried to make his voice sound as nearly like a woman's as he could so he could pretend that he was Eve. "We can eat from any of the trees here in the Garden except from the Tree of the Knowledge of Good and Evil. God told us not to eat from it, or even touch it, or we would die."

Returning to using his own voice, he finished the story about how evil came into the world. "When the woman believed Satan's lie that the tree was good for food, and because it looked so good, and because she believed it when Satan told her that it would make her wise, she took one of the tree's fruits and ate part of it. She also gave the fruit to Adam and he ate some of it, too. Then they recognized that they had done wrong. They had disobeyed God by believing what Satan told them and following what he said, rather than believing God and doing what He told them to do."

Shaking his head, Grandpa added sadly, "Because sin became part of their lives, almost like a virus it became part of their children's lives. And their children's children's lives, too. And sin has become part of the life of everyone ever since then."

"But that seems unfair!" Joshua said in a very upset tone of voice as he jumped up from the chair in which he had been sitting and listening. "I want to learn more about God and do what He wants me to. I really do. And that just doesn't seem fair to me. There should be a way to change it! You told me God is good! And I thought you said He's fair, too. Why should I have to do wrong just because two people did wrong way, way back when the earth and the stars and everything was so new?"

Josh was almost shouting and had tears in his eyes. He was shocked when he saw that his Grandfather and Grandmother had huge smiles on their faces.

"It's not funny!" he protested.

"Joshua, we're not laughing at you. We're smiling because what you're upset about has already been taken care of. That's what the New Testament, the second part of the Bible, is all about," Grandpa told him.

Immediately Joshua's whole attitude changed. "Really? Honestly? What happened?"

"God loved us so much that He already had a plan for what to do when Adam and Eve disobeyed Him. However, I think Grandma's got those waffles ready and waiting for us. And I think I see blueberries peeking out of them. So why don't we just wait until later to talk about that plan."

"Okay, but I can hardly wait to learn about it," Josh said. "I'm so glad to know God cared enough not to leave us without hope of being friends with Him. I've got a different question now, though. Can I try saying the prayer today?"

"That would be great," Grandpa said.

They all bowed their heads and closed their eyes as Joshua began, "Dear God, I haven't tried talking to you before so I'm not exactly sure how to do this, but thank you for these blueberry waffles. And for Grandma and Grandpa, and that plan I just heard about, that must be a good one. Thank you that I'm learning more about you every day. I can hardly wait for Mom and Dad to learn, too. Amen."

CHAPTER 7

PICKING STRAWBERRIES

Two small kittens lay sleeping under the shade of a large, old tree, while a beautiful Collie dog bounded across the driveway to greet Grandpa, Grandma and Joshua as they got out of their car at the berry farm. "How you doing, Laddie?" Grandpa greeted the dog as he patted his head. "You remember us after all these years, don't you?" And Laddie's tail wagged back and forth as he welcomed the three of them.

Grandpa walked over to the small shed. "Hi, Tom! Looks like business is good this spring. We'd like to pick three or four quarts of strawberries this morning. Where would you like us to begin?"

Joshua glanced ahead of them and noticed a few people out in the field with small boxes beside them, squatting down beside short green plants. One man carried a box heaped full of bright red berries as he limped to the little shed where Tom greeted customers and used a fishing tackle box for a cash register.

Motioning to his right, Tom said, "I'm just opening that section today. The other one is pretty well picked over and I think you'll do better if you check this one out. If not, you just go right ahead and move over to where the other folks are finishing up."

"Thanks! Are you still allowing people to enjoy eating a few berries while they pick?"

"That's part of the pleasure," Tom replied. "I do believe if we didn't let folks do that a lot of people wouldn't even come to pick berries. Part of the enjoyment we get from growing these strawberries is seeing the pickers' smiles as they taste the berries fresh from the plants."

"We'll be back as soon as we've got all we want. See you then," Grandma said to Tom as they headed for the area he had pointed out to them.

Josh watched Grandma and Grandpa each take a quart-size box and bend down to begin picking. Then he did the same. He had only put a few berries into his box when he remembered that he was allowed to eat a few, too. The next one he saw was a lovely bright red all over and the largest one he had seen. After he picked it he carefully separated it from its green stem and bit it in two. Sweet, pulpy juice filled his mouth and he felt a little bit dribble down his chin. "Oh, this is sooo good," he thought, and he quickly finished the first half and popped the rest of the berry into his mouth. "That was the best strawberry I ever tasted," he decided.

Then he noticed that Grandma and Grandpa were both ahead of him, picking more berries than he had. "I'd better stop eating and enjoying and start picking and saving, or they will be teasing me big time," he told himself. He bent down again and picked berries as fast as he could without ruining them by pinching them too hard when he pulled them off the plant..

It didn't take much time for bending to change into squatting and then back again to bending for all three of them. Either position for a very long time was difficult, but changing back and forth helped a lot. And each of them popped a strawberry in his or her mouth every now and then just because they were so nice and sweet and juicy.

It must have been almost an hour before they decided they had enough. It may have been that they had enough berries. Or it could have been that they had enough of bending and squatting. Or possibly it was that they had enough strawberry juice on their fingers and faces and enough dirt on their clothes. But they had enough of whatever it was, so they returned to the small shed to pay Tom for the berries they had picked.

Tom measured the strawberries into a container and told them, "You've got a gallon of berries. That's a good morning's work. Looks like you've enjoyed tasting a few along the way, too. I'm glad to see that. A gallon of berries is four quarts. And the berries cost two dollars a quart, so that'll be eight dollars."

"They're well worth it, Tom. I think these are some of the best berries you've had yet," Grandpa said as he paid him. "They've always been delicious, but this year they're exceptionally good. Thanks so much. And have a blessed day."

"Thanks," Tom replied. "God has blessed us, with health and this business, and good people like you as customers. It's always so nice to see you. May you be blessed until we see each other again next year."

"Thank you. But we might not wait that long. We're going to take our grandson home the day after tomorrow and we'll probably share a couple of these quarts with his parents," Grandpa told him.

"Great. Have a good trip. And I'll hope to see you again soon, then."

As the three of them climbed into the car, Joshua spoke up. "Mom and Dad will love us bringing them some fresh strawberries. We don't have a farm near us where we can pick them. Did you pick those blueberries that you put in our waffles here, too?"

"No," Grandma said, "we got them at a store, just like you have to. Blueberries like cooler weather than we have here so they don't grow well this far south. Grandpa and I didn't grow up picking blueberries but we both grew up picking wild raspberries and blackberries. They're not real pleasant to pick, either, because they grow on taller bushes that have small thorns on them. We both think that strawberries make your back ache more when it comes to picking, but blackberries and raspberries hurt your fingers more. But all of those berries are worth the little bit of hurting when it comes time to eat them."

"What are we going to do with all these berries that you aren't taking to Mom and Dad?"

"This afternoon we'll spend some time separating them from their stems, and tonight we're going to do our old-fashioned thing for today, besides picking them. We're going to make a freezer full of hand-cranked homemade strawberry ice cream."

"Is that as good as the ice cream we buy in a store?" quizzed Joshua.

"No," Grandpa replied.

"Then why make it?"

"Ha! Ha! Ha! Ha! Ha!" Grandpa laughed. "It isn't as good. It's better!"

"Oh, Grandpa, you're such a joker," Joshua laughed in return. "I just love wondering what you're going to say or do next."

CHAPTER 8

HOMEMADE ICE CREAM

By the time they were ready to eat supper, they all decided hot dogs cooked on sticks over a campfire sounded good. They opened a bag of vegetable chips, warmed a can of pork and beans over the fire, and had an at-home picnic ready in minutes. "Not the healthiest meal we've had," Grandma fussed, "but I'll let us get by with it this time."

As they ate, Grandma had an idea that Grandpa and Joshua really liked. "How about the two of you playing a game of horseshoes while I mix up the ice cream recipe? Then both of you can crank the ice cream, and while we let it harden maybe the three of us could play a game of horseshoes."

"Yahoo!" Joshua responded.

"Sounds good to me, too," agreed Grandpa.

"I do believe you've gotten better at horseshoes while you've been here," Grandpa told Josh as they threw their second round of the game. "You're lifting the horseshoes higher before you let go of them, and that helps them to go farther! Way to go!"

"Thanks, Grandpa. Guess I've been watching you and trying to do what I see you doing."

"Now that's a real compliment. Hope I can live up to it. That's not a bad idea for life as well as horseshoes. You can read about a Bible hero and study his life and learn to avoid his mistakes and follow his good points. Then read about another one and do the same thing. You'll find that Jesus is really the best hero of all because He never made a mistake. Learning what He taught and how He lived is the best example you'll ever find. When we talk about the New Testament you'll learn about Him, because everything in the New Testament has to do with Him in one way or another."

"Why not talk about it now?" Joshua asked as he picked up his next horseshoe and prepared to toss it.

"We could, but I think it might be better if we don't have horseshoes and homemade ice cream on our minds at the same time as that. God's plan is so wonderful that it's good to be able to understand and appreciate it instead of just paying a little bit of attention to it."

"Besides, I think you may have tied the score with that horseshoe you just threw. I want to see if I can keep you from beating me before Grandma brings the ice cream mix out here for us to crank," Grandpa added.

Grandpa tossed his last two horseshoes and they were figuring their scores just as Grandma appeared on the scene with the large bowl of strawberry ice cream mixture she had prepared. "Joshua, would you mind opening the camper door and reaching inside and to the right. There's a bag of salt there for us to use in making the ice cream. If you'd bring it here, we can get started."

"Salt? I never guessed that there's salt in ice cream," he said as he headed for the camper to get the bag.

"That's because there isn't salt in ice cream. This is a different kind of salt, the kind that you can put on your sidewalk and driveway if the weather is icy. You're going to be interested in seeing how it helps to make ice cream," Grandpa told him.

The ice cream churn was obviously old. The wood looked almost black in some places and quite worn in others. Some of the metal parts had rust on them, and the handle looked ready to be replaced. Grandpa said that only proved how much it had been used and appreciated. Grandma carefully poured the ice cream mixture she had made into the churn's inside metal container. Making sure that the container was tightly capped, with the post of the churn paddle, or dasher, poking through the hole in its cover, Grandpa settled it into the middle of the old churn. Then he packed ice around it, added a fist full of salt, put in more ice, added more salt, fastened the churn's handle section to the paddle post, and settled it securely on the churn.

"Slow and steady is the way to go, especially at first," advised Grandpa, turning the handle a few times and then offering the job to Joshua.

"How long does it take?" Joshua asked as he took over.

"Sometimes it might be fifteen minutes, other times it might be almost half an hour. I thought you and I could trade off every now and then until it's done."

"I think I'd buy one of those electric ones," Joshua said, rolling his eyes.

"Oh, no." Grandpa differed. "Part of the pleasure of making ice cream is the joy of slowing down if you've had a busy day. It gives you time to think about what the best part of your day was, or to decide what you might want to do tomorrow. Or you can just look around at other things. You know, like you did when we were canoeing."

As he cranked the ice cream churn for the next few minutes Joshua did just that. The first thing he noticed wasn't something he saw but something he could hear. Someone nearby was playing horseshoes, just like he and Grandpa had been. He could tell by the *clank* and *thud* as first one horseshoe and then another smacked against the horseshoe post and bounced or slid to the ground. Then he saw a colorful butterfly fluttering above a flowering bush. His eyes wandered from the hovering butterfly to the fluffy white clouds overhead. How white they looked against the beautiful blue sky. Amazing! All those things had been there before, but he hadn't noticed even one of them. Maybe the idea of taking time to look around at God's creation was something he could try doing more often, he thought.

"Did you notice how some water was coming out of this little hole here near the top of the churn, and how the ice level is getting lower?" Grandpa's voice interrupted Josh's musing. "That's from the salt melting the ice. Just like on an icy wintry sidewalk, the salt does its work. The ice melting in the churn allows the really cold water to completely surround the ice cream container. And as one of us turns the handle, the paddle inside the ice cream mixture keeps stirring it so it will freeze evenly."

After each of them had cranked the churn a little while, and Grandma had begged them to let her have a turn, too, Joshua was cranking again when he noticed something happening. "Uh-oh, I think something's going wrong with the freezer, Grandpa. It's getting harder and harder to turn."

"Oh, no, nothing's wrong with the churn. In fact, that's good news! It means the ice cream is very close to being ready to eat. Let me crank it a few times and see how much further it has to go," Grandpa said as Joshua stepped aside so his Grandfather could take over again.

"My goodness, you've almost finished our evening's work here. Not very long now until we'll be enjoying in a very delicious way some of those berries we picked." Grandpa gave the freezer handle a few final cranks, lifted the inner container from its briny bath, wiped it free of the salty water, and then removed the handle and crank from the churn.

Grandpa sat the dasher aside. "Oooh, doesn't that look good," Grandma almost purred, as Grandpa used a long-handled wood spoon and began to pack the ice cream down into the inner container. "Those little pieces of strawberry in with larger chunks of strawberry look just like I hoped they would," she added.

"Josh, would you run inside and get the cork on the kitchen counter?" Grandpa asked while he continued tamping down the ice cream. "I forgot to bring it out and we need it to plug the hole where the dasher was. Oh, and bring the folded blanket, too. We'll let this ice cream ripen while the three of us play that game of horseshoes we talked about earlier."

Like a flash Joshua was into the camper and back out with the cork and blanket. "Thanks," Grandpa said as he plugged the hole, added more ice and salt around the outside of their dessert-to-be, covered the top with the folded blanket, and set it under the shade of their large oak tree.

The three of them laughed and joked their way through a game of horseshoes that all of them agreed later wasn't nearly as exciting as they thought it would be. The thought of the ice cream was just too much of a distraction. The ice cream likely didn't ripen quite as long as it should have because they soon headed back to that freezer in the shade.

"I brought out some dishes that I put in the freezer earlier so our ice cream wouldn't melt so quickly," Grandma said as she scooped up generous amounts of the frozen pink confection for each of them.

"Aaaah!" "Perfect!" "Delicious!" "Delectable!" "The best ever! "Outstanding!" "Superb!" "Scrump-dilly-ish-ous!" If you can think of the way you would describe the best ice cream you've ever tasted, it's the word you would have used if you could have been there to have a dish of that strawberry ice cream. You probably would have asked them if you could have a second dish, too; and maybe even more than that.

It was as they were eating this simply perfect ice cream that Grandpa told Joshua the story he had been waiting to hear--a story that changed his life.

CHAPTER 9

FRIENDSHIP WITH GOD

"Do you remember when I told you about Adam and Eve?" Grandpa asked, as he ate the last bite of his second dish of the wonderfully delicious strawberry ice cream and set his dish and spoon aside.

"Yes, sir."

"Remember that God had given them a whole lot of good things to eat and only told them to avoid eating one thing?"

"Uh-huh. And they ate it anyway," Joshua said, glad that he could show his grandfather that he had been listening well earlier.

"Exactly! And that's really what sin is--choosing to do what we want to do rather than what God has told us to do. He told us not to do certain things because He knows what can hurt us or someone else. And it makes Him sad to see us doing things that cause pain to ourselves or to other people. That's why He sets limits. It's like your earthly father putting a fence around your yard if a vicious dog lives next door, and then telling you to be sure not to go outside that fence. You may not like being fenced in, but it's a lot better for you."

"I think I understand that Grandpa, but when I do wrong and feel bad about it didn't you say that keeps God from liking me?"

"God will always like you, and even love you. Please never forget that. But when you do wrong, or we could say when you sin, that sin separates you from God."

"But that's what I don't want to happen. That's the plan you talked about that I want to know about."

"It's like this," Grandpa said. "Since sin separates people from God, and God desires very much for every one of us to have a loving relationship with Him, He made a way for us to be close to Him again. His Son, Jesus, was willing to come to earth as a baby in human form. And when He grew up He taught people all around Him about God and what He was like and how God wanted them to live. He was very wise and caring, just like Father God is. Jesus did miracles, too, like taking a couple of fish and a few small loaves of bread, blessing and multiplying them, and then feeding thousands of people with them. And He healed people--like making a blind man see and a deaf man hear and a crippled person walk," Grandpa told Joshua.

"Cool!" Joshua said. "Everyone must have liked that. I'll bet He was the most popular guy around!"

"Not with everyone; for some people He became a problem. Some religious leaders didn't like Jesus being a better teacher than they were. He was good at using everyday things to help people understand more about God. Sometimes He would ask questions they would have to think about, and then they would learn even more. It made those leaders jealous and angry with Him. They didn't like it or believe it when Jesus said God was His Father. So they decided to come up with some kind of plan to kill Him."

"But God wouldn't let them do that, would He? I mean, you said God is strong. And you said He only does good things, so God wouldn't let them kill Jesus, would He?" Joshua protested.

"You know, I'm guessing that anyone living then who knew and followed Jesus must have thought just what you're saying. What they didn't understand was that it was necessary for Jesus to die so sin wouldn't keep us separated from God the Father," Grandpa explained.

"For more than a thousand years," Grandpa continued, "God had told His followers, the Jews, that for their sins to be forgiven they had to sacrifice a perfect animal. Only by the people shedding the blood of an animal, that had nothing at all wrong with it, could God accept their confession that they had sinned and not hold them guilty for it. The problem was that as soon as they sinned again, they had to live with feeling guilty all over again until another animal was sacrificed."

"How could Jesus' dying help?"

"Remember that Jesus knew when He came to earth that He was going to change things," Grandpa said. "By the life He lived, He tried to teach people about God and show how good and powerful and patient and wise and loving God is. But He also knew that He was going to die, to be a substitute for the animal sacrifices which people had been offering God for years for their sins. That's why, when they planned to kill Jesus, He wasn't surprised."

Grandpa paused to let Joshua think a moment.

Grandma continued with the story. "The night He was captured by His enemies, He even prayed that God might not let it happen. But then He told His heavenly Father that what He wanted most of all was for His

44

Father's will to be done. I think that must have pleased Father God very much. Jesus was much more concerned about making a way for people to be close to God again than He was about dying," she said.

"Oh, I bet that was hard. But how did they kill Him?" Joshua asked hesitantly. "How did He die?"

Grandma looked at Grandpa and he could tell that she wanted him to tell what happened next.

"After beating Jesus, spitting on Him, jamming a crown of thorns into His scalp, and dressing Him in royal robes to make fun of Him, they made Jesus carry His own rough, heavy cross up a hill. Finally, stripping Him to what back then amounted to His underwear, they nailed Him to the cross He had carried. And that's where He died."

"How awful!" Joshua cried.

"Yes, it was," Grandpa agreed.

"But there's more to the story," Grandma told Joshua, when she saw how sad he looked. "Jesus had told His disciples earlier that even though He was going to die, He would come to life again. They didn't think that could happen so, like you, they felt terrible. When a man who respected Jesus arranged for Him to be buried, His disciples didn't even stay around for His burial. Only the disciple John, Jesus' mother and a few other women had the courage to wait until He had died."

"Some friends they turned out to be," Joshua said.

"You're right. But you're also forgetting how forgiving God is," Grandpa said. "To go on with the story, there were guards set around the tomb Jesus was in, since some people were afraid His disciples might steal His body to try to make it look like He had come back to life. That was on Friday night. On Sunday morning there was an earthquake, and the stone that was closing the tomb was rolled away. When some friends and disciples looked into the tomb, guess what? Jesus wasn't there. He wasn't in there because He had come back to life, just like He said He would! If you've heard of the resurrection, that's what it was. It was Jesus being raised from the dead."

"Wow! What a great ending! I'm so glad He didn't stay dead! But where is He now?"

"In heaven, seated at the right hand of God the Father, where He's always praying for us."

"Awesome!" Joshua said with a contented look on his face. Then he tilted his head a little to one side and asked another question. "But how does that help me to be a friend with God? I don't get that part."

"God's plan was for Jesus to die for the sins of everyone. When a person recognizes that they do wrong, or in other words, they sin, they can ask Jesus to forgive them and be their Savior. If they have really meant it, they begin trying to live God's way instead of their own way. And that's the start of a wonderful friendship with God," Grandpa answered.

"It's that simple?"

"It sure is."

"Do you have to go to church to do it?

"No, God lets people make up their mind about it anytime and anywhere," Grandma said.

"How about here and now?" Joshua asked excitedly.

"We'd be delighted and proud," Grandpa replied. Before Grandpa or Grandma could even tell him what to do, Joshua began to pray.

"God, I'm so sorry people treated your Son, Jesus, like they did. But I'm so glad He was willing to die for people and didn't change His mind. It's cool that He was willing to do Your will and not His own. I really thank You for Your plan. I'm glad I can let You know that I'm sorry when I do wrong. I know I've done wrong. Please forgive me for sinning. I really want to live like You want me to. Thank you, God. In Jesus' name. Amen."

When he opened his eyes Joshua was surprised to see Grandma wiping her eyes. He thought he saw tears in his grandpa's eyes, too. "Did I do it wrong?" he asked.

"No, no," Grandma told him. "Some tears are tears of joy, and that's what these are."

"I thought that ice cream was great," Grandpa said, "but this is even better. We couldn't have had a more perfect night."

With a song in their hearts and smiles on their faces, they made sure the campfire was out, took the leftover ice cream and dirty dishes into the camper, and went to their beds with thankful, joyful hearts.

CHAPTER 10

MORE OLD-FASHIONED FUN

"Joshua, dear, it's time to wake up. this your last day here and we didn't think you'd want to use any more of your time sleeping." It was Grandma's voice he heard, though at first it seemed to be part of a dream he was having. "Joshua, wake up! It's ten o'clock!"

"Ten o'clock! How did I sleep that long?" Joshua asked as he sat straight up in bed. "I always wake up early. Give me a minute and I'll be right out." In a flash he was out of his pajamas, into his blue jeans and T-shirt, and making the few moves needed to get to the kitchen with a hop, a skip, and a jump.

"Wow! I'll bet you've both finished reading in your Bibles and praying. Did you eat without me?"

"We both had our coffee, but we decided we'd like to wait and have cold cereal with you since we're getting a rather late start on the day," Grandpa said as he tousled Joshua's already messy hair.

Each one prepared his own easy-to-fix breakfast and after a short prayer of thanks they all ate while they talked about what they would do on this last day together. "Have you ever played shuffleboard?" Grandpa asked.

"And have you ever ridden on a bicycle built for two?" Grandma questioned.

"No, I haven't done either of those things. I can ride a bike, but I don't know if I could ride one that's made for two people."

With a hearty laugh Grandpa said that he'd be glad to ride with Joshua on an old-fashioned bicycle made for two people if he would like to give it a try. Joshua reckoned that he would rather play shuffleboard, since he had never gotten to try that either.

"Oh, you don't have to decide between them," Grandma told him. "How would you like it if you and I played shuffleboard this morning while it's not too hot, since there's no shade over the shuffleboard courts? Then this afternoon you and Grandpa could ride one of those bikes around the shadier parts of the campground."

"Sounds good to me," Joshua said as he carried his dishes to the sink. "Let me brush my teeth and I'll be ready to go."

It wasn't a long walk to the shuffleboard courts. That was one of the blessings of summering here. It wasn't a large campground and nothing was so far away that you couldn't easily walk to get there. Before they began playing, Grandma warned Joshua that she wasn't much better at this than she was at playing horseshoes. At least she knew enough to be able to explain how to play it. No one else was there to see their mistakes, so they could laugh at themselves and with each other.

Joshua had to admit it was already almost too hot to play, but he enjoyed learning a few things about shuffleboard. After about a half-an-hour they both decided that the sun was just too warm, so they put away the equipment and headed home. "The nice thing about quitting now is that neither of us had to be a loser," Joshua said with a laugh. "Wait until Grandpa asks who lost. We can both say, 'Not I.'"

It was a lazy day. The sun blazed hot until evening, and even though Grandpa and Joshua had fun sharing their ride on an old-fashioned bicycle built for two, the heat kept them from wanting to spend much time doing even that.

"Seems to me if we're going to be doing anything active at all maybe it should be more like swimming," Grandpa suggested. The three of them changed into their swimsuits and went to the park's indoor pool.

"A-a-a-h, at last," Grandpa sighed as he floated on his back in the clear, cool water. But the next thing he knew Joshua had taken a dive underneath him with the idea of surprising Grandma by splashing her from behind. Unfortunately, Grandpa was between them and got even more of a surprise than Grandma because she turned and splashed Joshua back big-time. Soon, the three of them were diving and splashing like a trio of porpoises.

Grandpa had once been on a swim team and Grandma had been a lifeguard, so they were quite at home in the water. "Can you do this?" one of them would challenge the other, and then demonstrate a tuck or turn. And as soon as Joshua would try it, the other one would ask him if he knew a different swimming stroke or dive and show him how it was done. It was a wild, hilarious time as they romped together until they were almost worn out.

"We'd better save a little energy for tonight," Grandma suggested, as she climbed from the pool and toweled herself off. Joshua and Grandpa appeared reluctant to follow.

"What's going on tonight?" Joshua and Grandpa both asked.

"Oh, the campground is having a potluck supper."

"Pot luck? What kind of a meal is that? How can a pot have luck?" Joshua asked as he followed Grandpa in climbing out of the pool.

"It's funny how you use words for years and know what they mean, but you don't think about how they sound to people who have never heard them," Grandma said with a smile. "I don't know for sure, but I'm guessing that the name for the meal must have started long ago when people got together in hard times to share their food and just encourage one another by being together. Anyway, a potluck is when people cook something and then they bring what they've made to a place big enough for them to put the pots, or dishes, or platters on a counter or table. Then everyone fills their plates with whatever they would like to eat from all that's been brought."

"Oh, I get it! They have luck if what they like is in a pot that someone brought," Joshua exclaimed. "Is that our old-timey thing for today?"

"Well, we thought it would be our one old-fashioned thing. However, playing shuffleboard, riding a bicycle built for two people, and swimming all were a part of growing up that we both got to enjoy. Tonight after the potluck they've planned to play charades, which was a game our generation played, too. We thought you'd like to learn how to play it, too."

"That sounds like fun, but if you don't mind I'd rather we didn't stay for the charades, if it's okay with you," said Joshua.

"Have we worn you out today?"

"Oh, no! It's not that. It's just that I thought maybe we could play horseshoes again, and I'd love to look at the Big Dipper and The Queen and the other stars one last time before I go home. Don't forget about lightning bugs, either. You said I could take some fireflies home so I need to catch some of them, too."

"I'd choose Joshua's ideas over charades any day," Grandpa said enthusiastically, as he slid into his sandals, held open the door for Grandma and Joshua, and they headed for home.

CHAPTER 11

POTLUCK

"Sure smells good," Joshua commented a couple of hours later when they walked into the dining area of the clubhouse. As people began placing their dishes on the large table at one end of the room, he walked away from his grandparents and looked at all the food that was there. Everything he saw looked as though it would be something he'd like to eat. How would he ever choose from among them all? Fried chicken, mashed potatoes, green beans, corn on the cob, ham, sweet potatoes, the taco salad Grandma had brought, a spaghetti casserole, macaroni and cheese, tossed salad, three-bean salad, slaw, enchiladas, deviled eggs, pickled beets, and more. And there was another table that was just for desserts! He turned away from the big table and went over to see whether the desserts looked as yummy as the things on the first table did.

He didn't think he had ever seen so many temptations in one place. Angel food cake, chocolate cake, cherry pie, blueberry cheesecake, brownies, pound cake, apple pie, pecan pie, fresh fruit salad, a coconut pie, and all sorts of cookies. "Wow! What a feast!" he said as Grandpa walked up beside him.

"We thought you'd like coming to this," Grandpa said with a grin. "There's only one rule. You have to eat at least three things from the main table before you can head for the desserts. My suggestion would be that you don't eat so much that you have no room left for one final dish of that ice cream we made last night."

"No problem," Josh assured him, as they saw Grandma motioning for them to join her at one of the tables. They had just reached her side when the person in charge of the gathering asked everyone to join together in singing "God Bless America". A guitar played while everyone sang enthusiastically. Joshua was surprised to see that the guy playing the guitar was the man who had led the musicians the night they took their friendship walk. It felt good to see someone he felt he sort of knew.

As soon as the hymn was over, someone prayed for the meal. Then the people lined up at the two tables that were loaded with all the different things they had cooked and brought to share. One thing Joshua noticed was all the happy chatter, like when they were together for the time of singing a few nights earlier. The sounds of laughter and sharing blended with the delightful aromas of the many different foods and created a mixture of pleasure that everyone there seemed to enjoy.

It's a good thing that Grandpa had told Joshua that they would be having some of their own wonderful homemade ice cream later that evening or he might have eaten way too much. He didn't remember when he had wanted so much to eat at least a little bit of everything he saw. He did hold back enough at the big table that he still had room for a piece of that chocolate cake with caramel icing. M-m-m-m good!

Saying their good-byes to the people they had visited with while eating, they threw away the paper plates they had used, picked up the empty dish from the taco salad they had brought, and headed for home to their game of horseshoes, and one last dish of that scrump-dilly-ish-ous ice cream.

CHAPTER 12

SMILE, JESUS LOVES YOU

The fireflies were just beginning to show up and show off their talents as Grandma, Grandpa and Joshua arrived home. "I want to try to catch a few lightning bugs before we play horseshoes," Joshua said. "That way I'll be sure not to forget."

"I'm guessing you wouldn't forget," Grandma said with a playful smile. "I found a glass jar that I think should be just right for you. Grandpa has already punched some small holes in the lid. Go ahead and pull a little bit of grass to put in it so they'll feel more at home, and you'll be ready to start catching them."

It didn't take long for Joshua to capture several of these small bugs that fascinated him with the way each of them flashed off and on like twinkling Christmas tree lights. As he looked closely at one which he held in the palm of his hand, it lit up. He marveled at its being able to do that. "How do you suppose that happens?" he asked.

"I suppose some scientist could tell you how, but we sure don't know. We just thank God for all the different things He's put on this earth that we find pleasure in. We think of them as reminders of His wisdom and power and love," Grandpa answered.

"How does a lightning bug make you think of God's love?" Joshua asked with surprise.

"You know, God could have made a black-and-white world, but He made it colorful. And He could have made a world without bugs, I'm sure. Yet He chose to use even something as small as this to make His creation even more interesting for us. That's a way He shows His love for us. It's quite different from showing His love by sending Christ to die for our sins, but it's still love."

"Just like your hugging Grandma shows her you love her, but so does chopping vegetables with her, or watching her favorite TV show with her," Joshua suggested.

"Exactly," Grandma agreed as she gave him a hug.

"Aw, Grandma!" Joshua grinned as he put the last lightning bug he caught into his jar.

"Whenever you're ready for horseshoes, I have the game set up, so we can begin any time," Grandpa called.

"How about now?" Joshua asked as he sat the jar inside the back door and ran over to pick up one of the horseshoes.

One by one they took turns pitching as the *clank*s and *thud*s announced to the neighborhood that a game was going on. The day still hadn't cooled off a whole lot and one game was all it took for each of them to be quite willing to call it quits.

Just in case you wondered, Joshua came in second. Grandma and Grandpa didn't want you to know who won and who came in last, so we won't tell. But you can guess if you'd like to.

"Well, you've got your lightning bugs to take home and we've played horseshoes. I've forgotten what the other thing was that you wanted to do," Grandma said.

"I wanted to look at the Big Dipper and The Queen one more time, but I have a question about constellations first. Are there any more of those sky pictures like them, or are they the only ones?"

"Oh, there are many, many more constellations. Grandpa and I both used to know quite a few of them. To be honest, we've stopped looking for them and I've quite forgotten most of them but the Big Dipper and Cassiopeia. Over there the Big Dipper is," Grandma said as she pointed to the stars that were the outline of that very large dipper in the sky.

"Before you come back again," Grandpa assured him, "we'll refresh our memories so we can show you some more constellations next time."

"Well, I see the Big Dipper now and I had already spotted The Queen, so I hope I'll remember them the next time I see a dark sky," said Joshua. "You know, I felt sorry for you before, when I knew that when you were growing up you didn't have televisions or MP3 players or cell phones and all the things I've got. But I haven't missed those things while I've been here. Well, at least not much, anyway. Now I see that you had lots of good times without any of those things because you got to do all the fun things that we've done this week."

"But," he added thoughtfully, "lots of old people I see look so grouchy or sad, like they don't do any fun things or have any happy times. Why is that?"

"Well, lots of older people have problems with their health, or worries about not having enough money to pay bills, or are concerned about troubles their children or grandchildren have. That can take a lot of joy out of life," Grandma said.

"Well, I know Grandpa has a heart problem, and you've got lots of allergies, Grandma, and you both have hearing problems and wear glasses, and I don't think you have lots of money, but you haven't gotten grumpy. Why have they?" he argued.

"You know those smiley faces that you can add when you're e-mailing your friends?" Grandpa queried.

Joshua nodded.

"Way back in the late 1970's or '80's when those were new, you sometimes saw a smiley face with the expression, 'Smile, Jesus Loves You'. We asked Jesus into our hearts at about that time and we decided that it would be a pretty good way to live. Since then, as we read the Bible over and over, we noticed that almost two thousand years before there were smiley faces God had made the suggestion to think about good things. Paul, who wrote a lot of what's in the New Testament, wrote a letter while he was in chains in a prison, telling people to think about the things that are true and honorable and right and pure and beautiful and respected. Of course when you think about those kinds of things they bring a smile to your face, because they are reminders of God and His love," Grandpa said.

Grandma spoke up, too. "Even way back when King David was alive in Old Testament times, he wrote a lot of songs, called psalms, which encouraged people to praise the Lord. He gave them lots and lots of reasons to do that. He told them about God's greatness, and His goodness. He also reminded them of the beautiful and amazing things God had created, like animals and the foods that grow in the fields. Sometimes he wrote about the fact that God listens to them and loves them. All those ideas, and so many more things God does for us, should bring a smile to our faces if we think about them much at all. So we decided that 'Smile, God Loves You' would be a good way for us to live our lives. It's just another way of saying we would try to have an attitude of gratitude," she explained.

"Let me add one more thing," Grandpa said. "It's not always easy. Maybe you're not feeling well, or your best friend just found out they're going to have to move away, or you need an expensive car repair. Then your mind wants to focus on the problem. That's when you have to ask God to help you control your thoughts. Have you ever been on a runaway horse?"

"Huh? Why are you asking me about horses when we're talking about this? I don't get it," Joshua asked with confusion.

"Give me a minute and I think you'll see the connection. But tell me, have you ever been on a runaway horse?"

"Yeah, one time. He was okay going away from the barn, but when I turned him to go back to the barn, he began galloping so fast I was totally freaked out."

"What did you do?"

"I pulled back on the reins as hard as I could but he still kept running. If I hadn't ducked when he was going back through the barn door, I would have really got hurt big time."

"But you did think to pull back on the reins. That was important. Since you weren't old enough to have a lot of strength, he didn't respond to you, but if you had been stronger, he would have stopped. When we find our minds running away and not obeying what we know is the best way for them to be going, we have to treat them like that runaway horse and stop them."

"But remember, Grandpa, I couldn't stop the horse. What if my mind keeps going?"

"That's where prayer and the Bible come in. You just ask God to help you stop your mind. God is powerful, remember? You can also build up your spiritual muscles by memorizing verses that will help you rein in your mind. Together, you and God can do it. That's the kind of thing Paul meant when he wrote, 'I can do all things through Christ who gives me strength.'"

While Grandpa and Joshua were talking, Grandma had gone into the house and filled three small dishes with their ice cream left over from the night before. She brought them out and gave them each a dish as Joshua said, "I'm really glad you could answer my questions about God and that you told me about Jesus. And I--oh, no!"

"What's the problem?" Grandpa asked.

"I just thought about Mom and Dad and Gabe. I want them to know about what I've learned about Jesus and God, too. Do I know all I need to know now? Or is that like the constellations? Are there more things I can learn?"

"Would you believe that Grandma and I are still learning? That may sound like there must be more than you will ever want to know, but when you go home and find a good church you'll learn in fun ways, like Bible games and songs. At church you'll make other friends who want to learn, too," Grandpa answered. "And it's likely that as you pray for your mom and dad and Gabe, and discover what the Bible teaches, you'll get ideas about how to tell them. You might want to invite them to programs you'll be in or sometimes just ask if they'd like to go to church with you."

"And while we don't have a lot of your electronic things," Grandma spoke up, "we do have a computer and know how to email, and we do have a cell phone. That means there are ways that you can ask us questions if you need to. Or, if you just want to call and talk, we can do that, too. I know this is changing the subject, but would either of you like any more ice cream?"

With that Grandpa stood up, stretched, rubbed his stomach and said, "No, thank you. I don't think there's room in there for even one more bite, no matter how good it is."

"Me either, thanks," Joshua agreed. "Anyway, that will give the two of you a little ice cream to come back to tomorrow after you take me home."

"Before we go inside for the night, why don't we take a little time to thank God," Grandpa suggested.

"Sounds good to me," Joshua agreed.

"Me, too," Grandma said. Joining hands, they formed a small circle, bowed their heads and closed their eyes.

Grandpa prayed, "How thankful we are, Lord, for the beauty of your creation and the love you shower on us. We marvel at things like lightning bugs and we stand in awe that each thing you've put here on earth has a purpose. Thank you for giving us the Bible so we can learn about you and your love and your desires for our lives. How much you bless us, and we thank you for all that in Jesus' name. Amen."

Grandpa's *amen* was hardly out of his mouth when Joshua surprised his grandparents by adding his own prayer.

"Thank you, God, for all I'm learning about you. I'm so happy you forgive my sins because you want me to be your friend, and want to be my friend, too. How cool! Oh, and please, please help me be able to share all these awesome things with Gabe and Mom and Dad so they can know about you, too. Amen."

"Father, I am so thankful for our time with Joshua this week," Grandma prayed. "We've had so many fun times. And we're so thankful that he wants to know You better. Help him to find the right people to help him learn more from the Bible. And may he always have a heart to love and serve and please You. We love You *so* much, Lord. Amen."

With a beautiful, starry night above them, their tummies too full for even one more bite of that scrumptious ice cream, and hearts filled to the brim with thanks to God, they went inside and each had a night of pleasant dreams.

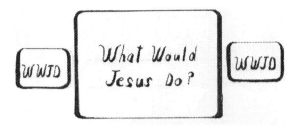

CHAPTER 13

WHAT WOULD JESUS DO?

For the first time that week, the sound of an alarm clock woke Joshua. "Today I go home," he thought, and he smiled as he pictured his arrival back home to hugs from his mom and dad. He could hardly wait to tell them about all he had seen and done and learned this week. Then he would jump on his bike and go see Gabe and some of his other friends. He knew he could text them, but he wanted them to see his lightning bugs. They would think the fireflies were as cool as he did.

He slid off the bed and out of his PJ's and got dressed for the day. As he tiptoed out of the room he saw that Grandma and Grandpa were already reading their Bibles. "We just read an interesting verse in Isaiah," Grandpa said. "I thought you might like to talk with us about it before we have breakfast. Would you?"

"Sure! What does it say?

Grandpa read aloud, "The LORD says, 'My thoughts are not like your thoughts. Your ways are not like My ways. Just as the heavens are higher than the earth, so are my ways higher than your ways and my thoughts higher than your thoughts.'"

"That's it?"

"Yep, that's it."

Joshua thought a little bit. "Well, I can understand the part about the heavens being higher than the earth, because we could see that real well on the nights when we looked at the stars. They look like they are real far from here. I'm not so sure that I understand about the thoughts and ways part of what you read, though."

"What you said about us looking at the stars is the kind of thing God was saying in that verse," Grandma encouraged him. "If you think of people here on earth and then picture God thinking thoughts about them, wouldn't you guess that what He thinks is much greater, or you could say higher, than anything people would come up with?"

"I guess so, because you told me the Bible says God is wise. And you also told me He's good and loving. And if He's like all that, His thoughts are better or greater or higher than how I think, that's for sure."

"Exactly. That would be true about the thoughts any person could think. God's thoughts would always be higher than theirs. That's also true about our ways. His ways are higher than people's ways, too."

"I don't think I get that part," Joshua admitted.

Grandpa was listening intently to the conversation. With a finger pointed at himself and then at Grandma, he asked Joshua a question. "You think we're pretty great, don't you?"

"Uh-huh. I sure do."

"Do you think we're perfect?"

"No, maybe not perfect, but you're close to it," Joshua answered fondly.

"Do you think that we never make a mistake, or sin?"

"No, as good as I think you both are, I know everyone makes mistakes and sometimes does wrong, even you."

Grandpa pursued Joshua with one more question. "Does God make mistakes? Does He ever sin?"

"You told me that He could only do right, and He couldn't tell a lie or break a promise."

"Does that help you understand that His ways aren't the same as our ways are?"

"Yeah, now I get it," Joshua admitted.

"When you get home and have to make up your mind about some things and aren't sure what to do, maybe it will help you to ask yourself an old-time question, WWJD, which means 'What Would Jesus Do?' You'll almost always notice that what you think He would do is a higher or better thing than many people would do. That will help you in making choices. That's our Bible study for this morning. We had our prayer time before you got up, so let's go fix breakfast, eat, and hit the road, okay?"

"Sounds good to me, though I still feel sort of full from last night. Would you believe it?"

They all agreed juice and toast was all the breakfast they wanted to have, so it didn't take long to fix it, eat, and get ready to leave. Joshua had already packed most of his things, and only had to get his jar of lightning bugs and gather up the few things he had brought along to have in case he got bored. "Guess I didn't need those at all," he thought as a big grin spread across his face. "Boring" was not a word that he had needed to use this past week.

CHAPTER 14

SHARING AND DREAMING

Three hours in the car passed rapidly with the singing, joking, and counting cars with out-of-state license plates. Joshua's hometown soon lay just ahead.

"Don't forget that we wanted to stop at a Christian bookstore before we go to their place, Honey," Grandma reminded Grandpa.

"Do you know where one is?" Grandpa asked Joshua.

"Oh, there's one at the mall we're just coming to. I've never been in it, but I've seen it. It's right beside the ice cream store. That's why I'm sure they've got one," Joshua laughed.

"I would suggest having an ice cream cone if I didn't know your mother's fixing lunch," Grandma said.

"Too soon for store-bought ice cream, anyway," Joshua stated. "After the strawberry ice cream we had this week, how can any other kind of ice cream taste really great again?"

"Now that's a compliment I'll remember for a long time, thank you!" Grandma said as they arrived at the mall.

Joshua led them to the Christian bookstore and proudly ushered them in. He was surprised to see all the things they sold. He had thought it would just have books, books, and more books, but there were pictures, toys, posters, lots of small electronics choices, a greeting card section, some T-shirts, games, and a bunch of other things. Of course, there were also books, books and more books, which is the section of the store Joshua noticed his grandparents heading toward.

He browsed around the different areas and then made his way to where Grandpa and Grandma were busily comparing one book with another. "You're just in time," they greeted him. "We want to buy you a Bible of your own so you can read the scriptures, too."

"Neat. Very cool. Thanks!"

After looking them over, Joshua chose a Bible from the three different Bibles his grandparents thought might interest him. They bought it and some thank you notes Grandma liked, and headed back to the car.

It was a short drive to Joshua's home. His parents must have been watching for their arrival because the minute they pulled into the driveway the front door flew open and both of his parents rushed out to greet them.

Joshua threw his car door open and leaped out as soon as the car came to a stop. "Mom! Dad! I've missed you. I had a wonderful time, but it's great to be home. I've got so much to tell you! We picked strawberries and made ice cream. We pitched horseshoes and went canoeing and did so many old-fashioned things. We saw lots of stars and--" Joshua stopped for a moment in the middle of his sentence, almost like he had stopped in mid-air when they were in the canoe. "And the coolest thing happened."

With a look of awe on his face, he continued, "I asked about the stars and Grandpa and Grandma told me about God creating them. The more questions I asked about God the more Grandpa and Grandma told me and I ended up asking Jesus to forgive me and come into my heart. And He's there now and I want to learn more about Him and they got me a Bible, and--"

"Whoa, slow down, son," his dad told him. "You've got lots of time to tell us all about your week. Let's take your things into the house first. We can hear more about things while we eat."

When they sat things down inside, the first thing Joshua grabbed was his jar of lightning bugs. "Look what I've got! Do you know what they are?" he asked.

"Lightning bugs!" both of his parents answered eagerly.

"I haven't seen fireflies for years," said his dad. "How great that you found some. I had almost forgotten that they even exist. I guess that I've been in the big city too long."

"And you said you picked strawberries," Joshua's mom said. "How nice that you could do that, too."

"We brought you some of them," Joshua told her excitedly.

"How would a strawberry pie sound?" his mother asked.

"I could help you; I've been helping Grandma and Grandpa to cook! Haven't I?" Joshua looked to them expectantly.

"He's been a great helper in the kitchen," Grandma said.

"And in lots of other ways, too," Grandpa added. "We're going to miss him."

They enjoyed their lunch while Joshua talked almost non-stop about all he had learned, and how he'd decided that life way back when Grandma and Grandpa were kids wasn't so bad after all. When they had finished eating, he jumped up and began helping to take the dirty dishes off the table. "I learned how to be part of a team whether we were canoeing or cooking or cleaning up. And guess what? It's neat to work together, like a team, just like when Gabe and my other friends and I play ball together."

"It sounds like maybe you did a little growing up this week," his dad observed.

"I'm also trying to learn how God would like me to live. Remembering to think about others before you think about yourself is part of that," Joshua said.

"Well, we'll certainly be interested in learning more about that," his mother said thoughtfully.

"Oh, that reminds me, since we talked with Joshua about God's character and about Christianity we thought it might be helpful for you if we wrote down some of the verses that refer to those things. Joshua has them in his suitcase," Grandma told her.

"Thanks for doing that. It may help. You know we haven't been going to church, and I'm not sure this will change our minds, but we won't discourage him if he wants to go. We just believe in letting him make up his own mind," Joshua's mom said.

"We can appreciate that. Of course, not knowing what Christianity is about would have given him little reason to decide in its favor. We just appreciate the fact that he is so interested in things around him. If he asks questions and there aren't verses about what he's talking about on the list he has, we'd be glad to have you call and we'll help all we can."

"Okay, Mom. Thanks! We might do that."

"We hate to eat and run, but we know you have tickets for the three of you to go to that ballgame tonight. Come to think of it, where did Joshua go? I want to be sure to give him a big goodbye hug before we leave. It's been such a joy to have him this week."

"That's good to hear. We wondered if he might almost be too much for you since you aren't used to having kids around anymore. I think the guys went outside so Dad and Joshua could see the GPS we bought yesterday. It will really be helpful when we get into parts of the city we're not familiar with, or when we take long trips," Joshua's mom said as she started toward the door so they could join the others.

It wasn't easy for Joshua to say goodbye, because he had had such a good time. At the same time, he still had so much he wanted to tell his mom and dad. And he wanted to go see Gabe, and his other friends, and share with them about the exciting things he had done and learned. They'd be amazed, like he was, to learn that life must have been fun even when there weren't all the great things they enjoyed playing with now. He hugged his Grandpa and Grandma and thanked them for his wonderful week. He was a little surprised to find himself holding back tears, even though he felt so happy.

"Goodbye," he called as they got in their car. "I love you! Thanks for everything."

"Goodbye," they echoed. "We love you, too! We love all three of you. Be sure to keep in touch," they called out as they waved to Joshua and his dad and mom. They fought back tears, too.

Grandpa started the engine and backed the car out of the driveway. Grandma reached her hand over and laid it gently on Grandpa's knee as they headed for home. "Goodbyes are so hard when it's someone you love so much. It really was a good week, though, don't you think?"

Grandpa reached down and squeezed her hand as he replied, "It was a wonderful week. Joshua's such a bright little boy with such a loving heart. I'm so glad God gave us lots of opportunities to answer his questions about God and Jesus. I look forward to seeing what the Lord's going to do in his life."

"I've already started thinking about what we might want to do next summer when he gets to spend time with us," Grandma said. "Maybe we could take a trip some place, like to a state or national park, and see some of the wonderful things God has made, like waterfalls, or geysers, or redwood trees, or a cave or two. God's made so many fantastically beautiful things. What would you think about enjoying some of them with Joshua? Wouldn't he make any trip even more special?"

Grandpa laughed a laugh of pure delight, thinking of all the possibilities. What fun they would have checking out different ideas and then deciding which one could be next summer's adventure for the three of them.

As they continued their drive homeward they thanked God for their wonderful week with Joshua and prayed for God to bless him as he told his friends and his mom and dad about his old-fashioned fun and his newfound faith. With hearts full of happiness because of the week just ending and dreams they were already starting to dream, they praised the Lord for the hope of more times for the three of them to laugh and love and learn together.

THE END

HOWEVER, if you would like to read the same verses that Joshua had in his suitcase for himself and his parents to read if they wanted to, they are in the Addendum, which comes next in this book.

Bye! And God Bless You.

ADDENDUM

Since you weren't there when Grandpa and Grandma talked with Joshua and had to read about those things instead, Grandma has listed the chapters where they talked about stories and ideas from the Bible. This is the same information she gave Joshua for his parents. You'll see that when there were a lot of verses she didn't type them all, but just showed where they (or you) could find and read the story. But when there were just one or two verses they are written here. There are many, many more stories and verses that could have been used, but this should be enough to get you off to a good start.

By the way, here's the Bible Grandma was using when she wrote the verses:

Scriptures quoted from *The Holy Bible, New Century Version*, Copyright © 1987, 1988, 1991 by Word Publishing, Dallas, Texas 75234. Used by permission.

It may be helpful for you to know that numbers given after the name of the book in the Bible will be written something like this:

John 3:16 First find the book of John (in the New Testament). Then the first number shows which chapter you need to look for, which in the example would be chapter three. And the number after the colon (:) is the verse you'll need to look for, which in this example would be verse 16.

If there's an "a" after the verse number it means only the first part of it is being quoted. If there's a "b" after the verse number it means the last part of that verse is all that's being quoted. One more thing: I'm going to put an NT before the book if it's in the New Testament or an OT if it's in the Old Testament. Your Bible doesn't do that, but I thought it might help you if you're new at this.

And now you're probably ready to read the information Joshua had in his suitcase to give to his mom and dad:

Chapter Two

Creation / OT: The story of creation, or how earth and the heavens were made and life began, can be read in chapters one and two of Genesis, the first book in the Bible.

Noah / OT In Genesis 6:5 – 8:22 you will find the story of Noah and the ark he built and the biggest flood ever.

Daniel / OT The story of Daniel in the lions' den can be found in Daniel 6:16-23.

Jesus / NT Stories of Jesus' birth, life, teachings, miracles, trials, death and resurrection are found in the New Testament in the books of Matthew, Mark, Luke, and John.

Creator / OT Isaiah 40:28a: "Surely you know, surely you have heard, the LORD is the God who lives forever, who created the world. . . ."

Creator / OT Ecclesiastes 12:1a: "Remember your Creator while you are young. . . ."

God made everything / NT John 1:3: "All things were made by him, and nothing was made without him."

God made everything / NT Colossians 1:16: "Through his power all things were made – things in heaven and on earth, things seen and unseen, all powers, authorities, lords and rulers. All things were made through Christ and for Christ."

Adam and Eve / OT You can read about how God made Adam and Eve in Genesis Chapter Three.

Heavenly Father / NT In the first book of the New Testament, Matthew, Jesus is teaching and in Matthew 6:9 he says, "So when you pray, you should pray like this: 'Our Father in heaven. . . .'" That tells us God is our Father in heaven, which is another way of saying he's our heavenly Father.

Heavenly Father / NT John 1:12: "But to all who did accept him and believe in him he gave the right to become children of God." If we are God's children, then God is our Father, and since we just learned he lives in heaven, again we recognize he is our heavenly Father.

God is good / OT Psalm 25:8: "The LORD is good and right; he points sinners to the right way."

God is Good / OT Nahum 1:7: "The LORD is good, giving protection in times of trouble. He knows who trusts in Him."

God is wise / OT Psalm 104:24: "LORD, you have made many things; with your wisdom you made them all. The earth is full of your riches." If you have wisdom it means you are wise.

God is wise / OT Daniel 2:20: "Praise God forever and ever, because He has wisdom and power."

God is patient / NT Romans 2:4: "He has been very kind and patient, waiting for you to change. Perhaps you do not understand that God is kind to you so you will change your hearts and lives."

God is patient / NT 2 Peter 3:9: "The Lord is not slow in doing what he promised - - the way some people understand slowness. But God is being patient with you. He does not want anyone to be lost, but he wants all people to change their hearts and lives."

God is just (fair) / OT Deuteronomy 32:4: "He is like a rock; what he does is perfect, and he is always fair. He is a faithful God who does no wrong, who is right and fair."

God is just (fair) / NT Romans 2:2: "God judges those who do wrong things, and we know that his judging is right."

God is forgiving / OT Nehemiah 9:17b: ". . . you are a forgiving God. You are kind and full of mercy. You do not become angry quickly, and you have great love. . . ."

God is forgiving / OT Psalm 86:5: "LORD, you are kind and forgiving and have great love for those who call to you."

God never lies or breaks a promise / NT Titus 1:2: "That faith and that knowledge come from the hope for life forever, which God promised to us before time began. And God cannot lie."

God never lies or breaks a promise / NT Hebrews 6:18: "These two things cannot change: God cannot lie when he makes a promise, and he cannot lie when he makes an oath. These things encourage us who came to God for safety. They give us strength to hold on to the hope we have been given."

God knows what's in our hearts / OT I Samuel 16:7b: ". . . God does not see the same way people see. People look at the outside of a person, but the LORD looks at the heart."

God knows what's in our hearts / OT Jeremiah 17:10: "But I, the LORD, look into a person's heart and test the mind. So I can decide what each one deserves; I can give each one the right payment for what he does."

Chapter Three

God made good things / OT During Creation how did God describe what he made? Genesis 1:10, 12, 18, 21, 25, 31

Chapter Four

God listens to prayer / OT Jeremiah 29:12: "Then you will call my name. You will come to me and pray to me, and I will listen to you."

God listens to prayer / OT Jeremiah 33:3: ". . . pray to me, and I will answer you. I will tell you important secrets you have never heard before."

Chapter Five

God's Word is a lamp and a light / OT Psalm 119:105: "Your word is like a lamp for my feet and a light for my path."

Chapter Six

God is wise / OT Psalm 104:24: "LORD, you have made many things; with your wisdom you made them all. The earth is full of your riches."

God is wise / NT Romans 16:27: "To the only wise God be glory forever through Jesus Christ! Amen."

God disciplines (corrects) us / OT Deuteronomy 8:5: "Know in your heart that the LORD your God corrects you as a parent corrects a child."

God disciplines (corrects) us / OT Job 5:17,18: "The one whom God corrects is happy, so do not hate being corrected by the Almighty. God hurts, but he also bandages up; he injures, but his hands also heal."

Satan was an angel / OT In Isaiah 14:12-17 Satan is called the King of Babylon because the people of Israel had been captured and made slaves by the king who then ruled the country of Babylon. In the same way Satan had captured people's minds and souls and made them become like slaves to wrong, sinful ways. You'll see in the next verse what Jesus said about Satan's fall.

Satan was an angel / NT Luke 10:18: "Jesus said, 'I saw Satan fall like lightning from heaven.'"

Satan tempted Adam and Eve / OT You'll find this story in Genesis 3:1-16.

Chapter Seven

Blessings / A blessing could be called a gift from God. It could also describe what we pray for when we ask God to show favor to someone. And when we demonstrate our thanks and affection for God that is called blessing (or praising) him. Here are some verses that talk about blessings:

Blessings / NT Mark 10:16: "Then Jesus took the children in his arms, put his hands on them, and blessed them."

Blessings / NT 1 Peter 3:9: "Do not do wrong to repay a wrong, and do not insult to repay an insult. But repay with a blessing, because you yourselves were called to do this so that you might receive a blessing."

Blessings / OT Psalm 145:10: "LORD, everything you have made will praise you; those who belong to you will bless you.

Chapter Eight

Act like God's children and/or Bible heroes / NT Ephesians 5:1, 2a: " You are God's children whom he loves, so try to be like him. Live a life of love just as Christ loved us and gave himself for us. . ."

Act like God's children and/or Bible heroes / NT Several heroes were mentioned in chapter two (above). If you want to read about some more of them, quite a few are found in the New Testament in the 11th chapter of Hebrews.

Chapter Nine

God sets limits / OT The Ten Commandments are found in Exodus 20:1-17 and again in Deuteronomy 5:6-21. But in almost every book of the Bible there are suggestions and guidelines to help us live lives that will make us and those whose lives we touch happier. If you follow them you will also please God.

Jesus fed people / NT Jesus' feeding of 5,000 people is recorded in Matthew 14:13-20; Mark 6:32-44; Luke 9:11-17 and John 6:1-13.

Jesus heals a blind man / NT Mark 8:22-26 tells about a blind man being healed by Jesus when he was in Bethsaida, NT and John 9:1-12 relates the story of a different blind man he healed.

Jesus heals a deaf man / NT Mark 7:31-37 tells about Jesus helping this man to hear and speak clearly.

Jesus heals a paralyzed person / NT John 5:1-9 is where you'll find the story of this miracle.

Jesus called God his Father / NT Matthew 6:9: "So when you pray, you should pray like this: 'Our Father in heaven, may your name always be kept holy.'"

Jesus called God his Father / NT John 8:54: "Jesus answered, "If I give honor to myself, that honor is worth nothing. The One who gives me honor is my Father, and you say he is your God."

Chapter Eleven

God is powerful / OT I Chronicles 29:11: "LORD, you are great and powerful. You have glory, victory, and honor. Everything in heaven and on earth belongs to you. The kingdom belongs to you, LORD; you are the ruler over everything."

God is powerful / OT Jeremiah 32:17: "I am the LORD, the God of every person on the earth. Nothing is impossible for me."

God is love / NT I John 4:15,16: "Whoever confesses that Jesus is the Son of God has God living inside, and that person lives in God. And so we know the love that God has for us, and we trust that love. God is love. Those who live in love live in God, and God lives in them."

God is love / NT Jude 21: "Keep yourselves in God's love as you wait for the Lord Jesus Christ with his mercy to give you life forever."

Shedding of blood / NT Hebrews 9:12: "Christ entered the Most Holy Place only once – and for all time. He did not take with him the blood of goats and calves. His sacrifice was his own blood, and by it he set us free from sin forever."

Shedding of blood / NT Hebrews 9:22b: ". . . and sins cannot be forgiven without blood to show death."

Jesus wants God's will to be done / NT Matthew 6:10: "May your kingdom come and what you want be done, here on earth as it is in heaven."

Jesus wants God's will to be done / NT Luke 22:42: "Father, if you are willing, take away this cup of suffering. But do what you want, not what I want."

Think about good things / OT Psalm 89:15,16: "Happy are the people who know how to praise you. LORD, let them live in the light of your presence. In your name they rejoice and continually praise your goodness."

Think about good things / NT Philippians 4:8: ". . . think about the things that are good and worthy of praise. Think about the things that are true and honorable and right and pure and beautiful and respected."

Focus on godly things / NT 2 Corinthians 4:1: "We set our eyes not on what we see but on what we cannot see. What we see will last only a short time, but what we cannot see will last forever."

Focus on godly things / NT Colossians 3:2: "Think only about the things in heaven, not the things on earth."

Christ gives strength / NT Philippians 4:13: "I can do all things through Christ, because he gives me strength."

Christ gives strength / NT I Peter 4:11b: "Anyone who serves should serve with the strength God gives so that in everything God will be praised through Jesus Christ. Power and glory belong to him forever and ever. Amen."

We have a purpose / When we accept Christ we become a part of all those who have accepted him as their Savior, and together those people are often referred to in the New Testament as "the church." God has a purpose for his church, so as part of that church we are a part of that purpose. He also has a plan for each one of us. The next two verses help us see those purposes.

We have a purpose / OT Jeremiah 29:11: "I say this because I know what I am planning for you," says the LORD. "I have good plans for you, not plans to hurt you. I will give you hope and a good future."

We have a purpose / NT Ephesians 3:10-12: "His purpose was that through the church all the rulers and powers in the heavenly world will now know God's wisdom, which has so many forms. This agrees with the purpose God had since the beginning of time, and he carried out his plan through Christ Jesus our Lord. In Christ we can come before God with freedom and without fear."

Chapter Twelve

Quote from Isaiah / OT This quotation is Isaiah 55:8,9: "The LORD says, 'My thoughts are not like your thoughts, your ways are not like my ways. Just as the heavens are higher than the earth, so are my ways higher than your ways and my thoughts higher than your thoughts.'"

How to treat others / NT Luke 6:31: "Do to others what you would want them to do to you."

How to treat others How to treat others / There are many other places in the Bible that talk about relationships that are pleasing to God and people. In the Ten Commandments (see chapter nine in this Addendum) is a concise list that Jesus basically summed up in this verse in Luke. As you read the Bible, pray that God will help you be alert to how he wants you to treat others.

How to treat others / NT Ephesians 5:10 says: "Try to learn what pleases the Lord." If you learn and practice those things, your life will be pleasing to God and will also make life more pleasant for people around you. If you notice carefully, I think you will find it makes your life happier, too.

TELL ME ABOUT GOD, GRANDPA

About the Author, Shirley McCoy

How can you help small children feel loved and secure in a chaotic environment? That was the prevailing question the author encountered when she learned of a young family being shattered by the effects of illicit drug use by one of the parents. With the conviction that God and His word offer the antidote God prescribes, Shirley wrote this book. You don't need a somber situation to appreciate the questions addressed by this first-time author. Shirley answers them in a God-honoring way through a story kids will understand and enjoy.

Mrs. McCoy is a pastor's widow with a Bible college diploma. Between pastoral appointments, she and her husband spent time as house parents in children's homes and a maternity home. Shirley especially enjoys writing devotions and teaching from the Bible. Before becoming a Christian she worked as an administrative secretary and a court reporter. She has four children, seven grandchildren, and six great-grandchildren, and appreciates every opportunity God gives her to enjoy time with them talking about biblical answers for life's everyday problems.